What people are saying about …

The Meeting of the Waters

"Fritz Kling's book … should be basic reading not only for all Christians involved in global missions but also for any believers trying to reach out to their own city."

Tim Keller, senior minister of Redeemer
Presbyterian Church in New York City

"I'm glad that we have [Fritz] as a guide as we pioneer the next era of answering the Lord's call to each of us: to do justice, to love mercy, and to walk humbly with Him."

Gary Haugen, president and CEO of
International Justice Mission

"*The Meeting of the Waters* effectively communicates the issues that will shape mission strategies in the future. This is a book that should be read by … anyone committed to fulfilling the Great Commission as we move further into the twenty-first century."

Jerry Rankin, president of the International Mission
Board of the Southern Baptist Convention

"Fritz Kling's book is both refreshing and powerful.… You do not have to agree with all of his reflections, assertions, and conclusions, but you must face squarely the questions Fritz raises, questions imbedded in rich stories accessible to any reader concerned with the global church."

The Right Reverend Doctor D. Zac Niringiye,
assistant bishop of the Kampala Diocese,
the Church of Uganda (Anglican)

"The twenty-first-century world is changing at a dizzying pace.... This book is a must-read for Christians who want to stay relevant and effective."

Richard Stearns, president of World Vision
U.S. and author of *The Hole in Our Gospel*

"In *The Meeting of the Waters,* Fritz Kling offers a highly relevant response to one of the central questions of the twenty-first century: Is religion going to be a barrier of division, a bomb of destruction, or a bridge of cooperation? By connecting Sundays to the rest of the week—the institution of the church to the world of diversity—Fritz Kling is showing us how to build a bridge."

Dr. Eboo Patel, executive director
of Interfaith Youth Core

"*The Meeting of the Waters* is the most significant book on international mission I have come across in a long time and one that echoes my own observations. Fritz Kling has the skinny on the movements that are impacting the changing landscape of Christian mission. This book is the result of thorough research in a broad sweep of mission situations, and the results are both enlightening and challenging. I highly recommend this book for those who want to know what mission in the real world actually looks like."

Andrew Jones, director of the Boaz
Project, http://tallskinnykiwi.com

"Fritz Kling … helps the reader access the parallel streams of our unidirectional past and the globalized, multidirectional future. Meet Fritz's friends, colleagues, and acquaintances around the globe, who guide the reader into and through the all-bets-are-off global environment."

Rodolpho Carrasco, U.S. urban ministry veteran, Alumni Hall of Fame member of the Hispanic Scholarship Fund, Christian Vision Project contributor, and board member of World Vision U.S.

"This is an astonishing book…. Highly recommended."

Davis Bunn, best-selling author of *Gold Of Kings*

"This is a call to action we all need to read and enact."

Mark Siljander, PhD, former member of the U.S. Congress, U.S. ambassador to the United Nations, and author of *A Deadly Misunderstanding*

The Meeting of the Waters

The Meeting of the Waters, Manaus, Brazil

The Meeting *of the* Waters

7 Global Currents
That Will Propel
the Future Church

FRITZ KLING

David C Cook®
transforming lives together

THE MEETING OF THE WATERS
Published by David C. Cook
4050 Lee Vance View
Colorado Springs, CO 80918 U.S.A.

David C. Cook Distribution Canada
55 Woodslee Avenue, Paris, Ontario, Canada N3L 3E5

David C. Cook U.K., Kingsway Communications
Eastbourne, East Sussex BN23 6NT, England

David C. Cook and the graphic circle C logo
are registered trademarks of Cook Communications Ministries.

The Web site addresses recommended throughout this book are offered as a
resource to you. These Web sites are not intended in any way to be or imply an
endorsement on the part of David C. Cook, nor do we vouch for their content.

Many of the names mentioned throughout this book
have been changed for privacy purposes.

All Scripture quotations, unless otherwise noted, are taken from the *Holy Bible, New
International Version*®. *NIV*®. Copyright © 1973, 1978, 1984 by International Bible Society.
Used by permission of Zondervan. All rights reserved. Scripture quotations marked NRSV
are taken from the New Revised Standard Version (Anglicized Edition), copyright 1989,
1995 by the Division of Christian Education of the National Council of the Churches of
Christ in the United States of America. Used by permission. All rights reserved. Scripture
quotations marked NASB are taken from the *New American Standard Bible,* © Copyright
1960, 1995 by The Lockman Foundation. Used by permission. Scripture quotations
marked KJV are taken from the King James Version of the Bible. (Public Domain.)

LCCN 2009942956
ISBN 978-1-4347-6484-3
eISBN 978-0-7814-0429-7

© 2010 Fritz Kling
Published in association with the Eames Literary Services (LLC), Nashville, TN.

The Team: John Blase, Sarah Schultz Caitlyn York, Karen Athen
Cover Design: Amy Kiechlin
Cover Image: iStockphoto, royalty-free

Printed in the United States of America
First Edition 2010

1 2 3 4 5 6 7 8 9 10

123009

*To Val—impossibly gracious, beautiful, and
bright, ever the Lady to my Tramp.*

—————

*To Jack and Marilyn, whose youthful joy in
helping others is a life model for me.*

—————

*To Jerry and to Deana, who hired me to implement
their world vision before I had any.*

—————

*To thousands of mentors who patiently
taught me most of what I know.*

Contents

Foreword

Refreshing and powerful! That's how I describe Fritz Kling's book *The Meeting of the Waters*. Fritz deals with theological and philosophical issues in a manner accessible to any reader—through story. He tells his own story coupled with the stories of others all over the world in a way that draws readers to reflect on their own stories. This book names our worlds—what Fritz calls the global church and the field of Christian mission—not in the traditional territorial and socioeconomic categories of reached and unreached, the West and the rest, but with deeper, more intriguing and inclusive characterizations.

The seven Currents presented in this book are realities common to all—whoever we are, irrespective of ethno-racial identity; wherever we are, North, South, East, or West; and whatever socioeconomic class we belong to. They also strike at the heart of the message of the gospel and presence of the kingdom of God in our world. You may not agree with all of his reflections, assertions, and conclusions, but I believe you must squarely face the questions he raises, questions vital to discussions of individual discipleship and the global church. I cannot say enough about Fritz's honesty. While acknowledging the blessing of his Euro-American heritage and experience, he also admits its pitfalls and inadequacies. Fritz is the first to admit that this heritage skewed his understanding of the gospel and Christian mission. He sets an example for us all to be self-critical and embrace perspectives of our brothers and sisters living in different cultures and economies in order to further the influence of the gospel and the global church.

The Right Reverend Doctor D. Zac Niringiye,
Assistant Bishop, Kampala Diocese, the
Church of Uganda (Anglican)

Introduction

Mission Marm and Apple Guy

It was 2:00 a.m., and the knocking on the locked iron door was getting louder. It kept coming as I slid out of bed, stumbled in the dark to the door, and groped for the big ring of keys hanging on the wall.

I was groggy from the overnight flights from Richmond to Miami to São Paolo to Manaus, Brazil. Manaus used to be the capital of the world's rubber industry and is now a gritty, gateway city into the Amazon Basin for tourists, business people ... and missionaries. People like me.

While I was in Manaus, I found myself sleeping in a missionary jungle pilot's basement bunkhouse. I finally opened the heavy iron door to a missionary woman in her sixties, and I thought I was dreaming. It was my aunt Vera.

There was one problem: Aunt Vera had been dead for more than twenty years. But the woman standing before me was a dead ringer for my dead aunt. Like Aunt Vera, she wore her grey hair in a bun, bifocal glasses on a leash, an ankle-length print dress, and sturdy shoes. It had been more than sixty years since Vera had gone to serve the Lord in Iran, but the missionary lady at the door bore an uncanny resemblance to my aunt.

When she returned from Iran, my real aunt Vera had become what they used to call a schoolmarm—"a woman teacher, especially one who is regarded as strict."[1] That is why I immediately thought of my late-night visitor as Mission Marm. I believe that everyone involved with Christian ministry around the world knows a Mission Marm.

As she stood in the doorway, Mission Marm had the steely-eyed gaze and brusque manner of a woman who had lived alone in developing countries for decades. Her bone-crushing handshake betrayed years, I guessed, of laying bricks, delivering babies, sewing clothes, and farming. I would love to reflect on our conversation and what I learned about her life in the mission field … except that we barely spoke. I am by nature a questioner; she was a woman of few words. She walked past me, down the hallway to one of the vacant rooms.

I later pieced together her story. Mission Marm became a missionary in the 1970s, at a time when America was an isolated player on the Cold War stage. China and Russia were closed to foreigners. She, like Aunt Vera, knew she would only see "home" about every five years, so she loaded a steamer trunk and boarded a ship or plane for her trip to "the field." Communication was only by sporadic mail service. The need was serious, the conditions harsh, and even a lifetime of evangelization seemed too short for the task.

After our brief meeting, I could tell that Mission Marm had probably forgotten more about Christian service than I had ever known. Her devotion, experience, and resolve were palpable; this woman twenty-five years my senior barnstormed around the Amazon Basin all day and night.

I was in the missionary bunkhouse because I run a Christian foundation, where my job is finding ways to invest in the growth of the global church. The global church is not a certain denomination or building, an individual mission agency, congregation, or megachurch. It is informal and undefined, not bound by a specific nation. If I were to try for a concise definition of "global church" I would say,

The community of followers of Christ, heeding

His call to be His arms, legs, and voice around
the world.[2]

Neither an institution nor a bureaucracy, the global church is incredibly adaptive and vibrant. It has long been the world's most effective relief agent, meeting needs across the globe through justice advocacy, material aid, counseling, biblical proclamation, education, and more.

I know that from personal experience. Over the last ten years I have visited over forty countries, met with a few thousand ministry leaders, and bounced through hundreds of hours in vans to project sites. I have downed gallons of coffee, Coke, and chai served up by my hosts in places where they knew I could not drink the water. During my travels, I have walked where Jesuit missionary Matteo Ricci walked in sixteenth-century China. I have accompanied an Australian nurse as she tended to the elderly in an Asian leper village. I have learned from Russian preachers who were jailed during communist times. I have been spellbound by Ugandan underground church pastors as they described private audiences with heinous strongman Idi Amin.

During those years, I have also had the privilege of meeting hundreds of people like Mission Marm. These people are my heroes. I find it impossible not to feel humbled and grateful seeing firsthand the sacrifices and fruit of past Christian workers' efforts. In difficult years past, missionaries left port for their assigned country with their belongings packed in coffins, fully expecting to live out their days in their new country. I can relate to 1950s U.S. statesman Adlai Stevenson who, after visiting mission stations in Africa, was asked about what impressed him most. "The graves," he said. "At every mission station there were graves."[3]

Just after drifting back to sleep, I was reawakened at 4:00 a.m. by the rattling of the iron window bars. I felt like I was bunking in an equatorial Underground Railroad, with unknown travelers drifting through at all hours on their way to one part or another of Latin America. This time I opened the door to a man in his late twenties, en route to a remote jungle village to begin his new career as a teacher. Pleasant and casual, he immediately plopped down on the couch and multitasked while we talked. I watched him Facebook and send text messages to his family in Ohio, who were all most eager to know he was safe.

With his scruffy beard, T-shirt, baggy shorts, flip-flops, and compact technology, the man seemed like a typical twenty-first-century young adult. He reminded me of a sales associate in my local Apple store. I dubbed him Apple Guy.

"I was working as an engineer in the States when I traveled with my church to Brazil on a short-term mission trip a few years ago. That was when I 'caught the missions bug.' We did work at a mission school in Brazil's interior. After I returned home, I kept up with their newsletters and emails. It turned out that my wife and I really had a heart for the school and for Brazil."

Then the inevitable happened—history, global politics, and providence (not in that order) aligned to shape the future plans of Apple Guy, his church, and the mission school. "Brazil's government was becoming increasingly anti-American," he said, "and it began imposing more restrictions on American organizations." A large American mission agency had been providing staff to the school for a long time, and the government treated the agency as a high-profile scapegoat. So the agency decided to pull all of its personnel out of Brazil.

As Apple Guy spoke I knew, though he didn't, that this kind of missionary eviction was common around the world—just one more sign that mission times were changing.

However, the government needed Brazilian children to be educated, so in order to keep the school functioning they would find just one expatriate couple to replace the several who used to run the school.

Apple Guy concluded, "The school made its need known, and my wife and I prayed and talked to the kids about it. We decided to give it a shot—we would all move and run that boarding school in the interior of Brazil. I was as surprised as anyone!"

As he slouched into a couch, a series of photos of his children's happy faces shuffled across his laptop's screen. Finally, he pulled up a movie; he said it would help him fall asleep.

The two visitors could not have been more different.

- Mission Marm was single. Apple Guy would soon fly his family down to join him.

- Mission Marm was a lifer. Apple Guy had committed to three years, with an option to re-up.

- Mission Marm had responded to a life calling, and she had just this one career in her life. Apple Guy was on his third—and almost certainly not last—career, pursuing a change of vocation for a time.

- Mission Marm had studied and trained to be a missionary, and her whole working life had been in Christian service. Apple Guy had spent his working life in the secular workforce and expected that his mission stint would utilize the skills and vocational experience from his stateside job.

- Mission Marm had given up all of her Western accoutrements and conveniences to serve in any way or place that she was needed. Apple Guy brought his gadgets and toys with him to a place he had chosen.

- Mission Marm had begun her career taking furloughs back home a few times every decade. Apple Guy expected to return to the States every year, probably retain ownership of his house in the States, and certainly remain in constant email and phone contact. He and his family also knew they would be visited, annually or more often, by relatives and various short-term mission groups from back home.

That night in Manaus, I glimpsed the future: The global church was undergoing a generational changing of the guard. In a world of widespread upheaval of every kind, the global church was drifting between a storied past and a rapidly morphing future. Mission Marm was giving way to Apple Guy, and it wasn't a question of "when?" but "how?"

In coming years global church leaders will be able to employ some traditional approaches from the past, but they will increasingly need to try out experimental, innovative, and even uncomfortable ideas. A generation of Christian workers like Apple Guy will depart from Mission Marm's methods at almost every turn, which will lead the global church into uncharted waters.

But will that next generation be up to the task? Beyond the hip clothes and cool gadgets, will they bring enough depth and commitment to very difficult cross-cultural assignments? Are they prepared to minister and teach Christian faith to people in complex and changing cultures? Will Apple Guy and his contemporaries know how to forge relationships with leaders from less-developed, less-powerful countries? I know that Apple Guy cannot fulfill his task alone, but will older religious leaders allow his generation a place at "the adult table"?

As I thought about the generational shift, I wondered if the emerging generation's voice would be heeded. Would the global church of the future incorporate the new generation's focus on justice, relief, poverty, conservation, and mercy? Christian workers in the past often tended to focus on individual needs and spiritual concerns but, as a British journalist recently noted, young Christians today are "as concerned with ecology, AIDS ... and with human rights worldwide as with traditional questions of personal morality."[4] I felt certain that Mission Marm could not effectively advance those emerging concerns, but I also had my doubts about Apple Guy.

Right now, over 400,000 Christian missionaries are living in countries other than their own, carrying a message or delivering a service to the ends of the earth.[5] I am, wherever I go, almost a knee-jerk defender of the work of the Christian church around the world. The good work done by Christians over the years—the hospitals started and staffed, the schools built, the sick people treated, the science and agriculture taught, the souls saved—far eclipses any negative history. I work for American donors who help the Christian church serve the world. The last thing I want to see is disheartened or discouraged Christian workers, but I feel a need to express my concern.

You see, I believe that Mission Marm's days are waning; the future of the global church will look very different. Hockey great Wayne Gretzky is reputed to have explained why he always seemed to be the first player to the puck: "I don't skate to where the puck is; I skate to where the puck is going to be." I wondered, that night in the bunkhouse, if the global church was skating to where the puck was going to be.

Others share my concerns. I read a report by an international panel of church experts charging that, all too often, global church leaders do long-range planning as if the future is simply going to be an extension of the present. The report questioned whether the Christian church has the ability or desire to recognize a world in flux and figure out how to respond.[6] Another writer called for global church leaders to become "incredibly well-versed in the ways that globalization affects their particular field, [for] turning a blind eye to the issue is incredibly dangerous."[7] That is why I have written *The Meeting of the Waters*—to address the issues of globalization and the church head on.

I was in Manaus, Brazil to visit an aviation ministry that flies supplies and teachers to remote Amazon River villages. Since planes were the ministry's "business," the workers decided that an actual flight downriver would give me the best firsthand experience.

Early that morning I was picked up and driven to Manaus-Eduardo Gomes International Airport. I did indeed learn a few things about aviation ministry that day but, to my surprise, my greatest lessons were much more sweeping. What had been a lingering hunch about the church in the twenty-first century became for me a consuming quest.

As we flew over the sprawling port city and then countless river villages, I thought about Christian presence in those places below … and around the world. From the air, those remote villages looked just like they must have appeared one, two, or even three hundred years ago. On the ground, though, they were very different. Even as some villagers poled to and fro in dugout canoes, many others talked on cell phones to their friends and relatives in other river villages and cities.

I wondered whether either Mission Marm or Apple Guy would be effective in those river villages today. Or in cities like São Paolo, Bangkok, Phoenix, or even Manaus, for that matter. As those places morphed, I knew, so must Mission Marm and Apple Guy and the rest of the global church.

In our six-seater float plane, we touched down in several of the river villages to visit indigenous churches and pastors. We traipsed barefoot through knee-deep mud and muck and navigated rickety boardwalks between shacks on stilts, with ramps leading from the tied-up canoes and motorboats to the front door. We visited a church that met in a screened-in hut, which doubled as a community lodge where the village men watched soccer matches on satellite television. It might have been an Amazon River village, but it was still soccer-mad Brazil.

Flying back upriver to Manaus, our plane banked over the city to see a local landmark. In Manaus, two distinct eastbound rivers converge to form the fabled Amazon River, which then flows nearly one thousand miles until it reaches the Atlantic Ocean at Belem. Tourist brochures gush about the "Meeting of the Waters," but I confess to some indifference about tourist attractions. Over the years, I have visited about twenty different "seventh wonders of the world"—but this one lived up to its billing.

Like oil and water, the Amazon's two tributaries do not blend or mix upon meeting, but create instead a seam of sorts. They appear from the air to be side-by-side runners of black and caramel carpet. From my plane, I could see tour boats sitting astride the seam, with passengers on one side of the boat looking down at the placid Rio Negro, and people on the other side watching the caramel commotion of Rio Solimões.

The southern tributary, Rio Negro ("black water"), is the largest blackwater river in the world. It is tannic—the color of very dark tea or even wine—because upstream it cuts through forests of leaf-shedding trees. Rio Negro's water is dense and heavy, virtually free of mineral content and home to sparse fish life because it is so acidic. Though dark, it is also crystal clear.

The northern tributary, Rio Solimões ("white water"), is caramel colored and wavy, full of churning vegetation and silt from mountains in western South America. It has plentiful fish life. Faster moving than Rio Negro, Rio Solimões swirls, churns, and rushes toward the Atlantic.

At the Meeting of the Waters, not only is the seam dramatically visible from above, but it is also three-dimensional—almost as if an underwater wall or baffle rises from the riverbed to the surface of the water. A Brazilian missionary friend described diving into the river and swimming underwater from one stream into the other. She exhilarated in bursting through the underwater wall into the other stream.

For ten miles, as the newly formed Amazon courses east, the two rivers run completely distinct and separate in their shared channel. The seam visibly exists for that whole distance until, finally, the waters blend.

Looking down on the river and jungles, I listened to my pilot's fascinating running commentary and found myself thinking about his life in the heart of the Amazon ... and about hundreds of thousands of Christians like him serving around the world. The Meeting of the Waters, I thought, was a perfect metaphor for my previous night's realization about the global church at a crossroads.

Like one of those tour boats, the global church today sits at the confluence of two powerful streams. One is the past era, when the Christian church around the world relied upon dedicated Christians from North America or Europe. Those foreigners stayed for extended periods—years—at great expense; emphasizing personal piety, they were strong in the Bible, missions, and service. Mission Marm and her colleagues dedicated themselves to specific people groups or countries or regions and developed expertise there. They were focused on personal lives and spiritual things, and not on the world or global affairs.

The other stream represents the globalizing world with its changes that are spreading immediately and indiscriminately. That stream is evolving and unpredictable, and it cannot be ignored or dammed. It is characterized by conditions almost entirely different from those the church faced in eras past: different forms of transportation, speed, communication, entertainment, political forces, national and ethnic identities, culture, conflicts, crises, economies, and technologies. Most significantly, the new stream brings a completely scrambled roster of "players" and issues. People from all around the world are involved, with newfound voices of credibility and urgency. As a result, the future church will need to find its voice in a wider-than-ever range of issues, like poverty, human rights, ecology, justice, conflict, equality, reconciliation, and global events.

Amid all these changes, I am reminded of the warning of former General Electric chairman Jack Welch: "If the rate of change inside an organization is less than the rate of change outside … their end is in sight."[8] As a Christian, I take heart that the gospel story is blessedly different from the corporate world. God's Word will assuredly survive, and His truth will prevail in the end. My question, though, is not concerned with eternity; it is about today and tomorrow. How can Christians be faithful and relevant in these volatile, fluid days, as we seek to spread good news to people of different cultures in a winsome way?

Christians, I believe, have always struggled with whether to embrace or reject the world, but separatism is no longer an option. The admonition of British scholar John Stott rings truer now than ever. Dr. Stott charged world-concerned Christians with engaging in "double listening," paying attention "both to the ancient Word and to the modern world, in order to relate the one to the other with a combination of fidelity and sensitivity."[9]

The best leaders around the world—secular and Christian, in developed and developing nations—recognize the need to understand the changing world in order to remain viable in their own fields. Author Thomas Friedman writes, "In a world where we are all so much more interconnected, the ability to read the connections, and to connect the dots, is the real value added…. If you don't see the connections, you won't see the world."[10]

I believe the distinctions between how churches thrive and how the world does business are blurring. Christians seeking to understand the church's role in the future must be effective double listeners, like Stott, while connecting the dots, like Friedman.

Mission Marm, though, is ill suited for dot connecting. Decades ago, she left the world as she knew it and focused on a new culture. She dedicated herself to meeting the immediate needs of day-to-day people. I thank God for her. The day she boarded the ship, Mission Marm laid any hopes for keeping up—with friends, with news, with the world—on the altar. She went "back in time" then, and our brief meeting convinced me that she would never catch up again.

Apple Guy, on the other hand, hardly appears ready to take over the helm of the global church. He excels in double tasking, but he will surely have difficulty double listening. Flexible and capable of adapting, he likely lags in teaching skills, counseling, mission history, international experience, and ultimately perhaps, commitment.

So, on one side of the Meeting of the Waters is a familiar stream that allows the global church to be safe but stodgy. On the other side is a stream whose wild currents will move the church toward future relevance … and also risk and change. At this new and confusing juncture, church leaders must be forward thinking and bold in forging ahead, despite certain discomfort.

Just like the Meeting of the Waters, the global church's distinct streams are bound to merge in the coming years. In that newly globalized world, the long-standing methods and messages of Mission Marm and her generation will show their age. At some point, even the current approaches of Apple Guy will falter, for that future age will generate new needs and responses of its own.

Between the extremes of Mission Marm and Apple Guy is where most Christian workers reside: They seek to be relevant *and* orthodox, productive *and* faithful, current *and* grounded, innovative *and* contented … and often they simply end up feeling overwhelmed. Many followers of Christ who identify more with Mission Marm sense that the global church needs to change, and many Christian workers who relate to Apple Guy have the nagging sense that they are not fit to carry Mission Marm's bags.

The church, as it strives to reach future generations, will need to bundle Mission Marm's passion for evangelizing unreached people groups, Apple Guy's project-management skills, and countless other approaches that emerge for future societal changes.

This book provides the global church not with a one-size-fits-all map detailing the river's course, but a flexible and varied tool for continually recognizing and adjusting to the all-bets-are-off global environment. It is a tool that must be widely used and shared.

Tradition-minded church leaders accustomed to listening to the Word may be daunted by global realities they have not yet learned to read. At the same time, leaders doing ministry at the very cusp of the cutting edge may need to work harder at incorporating the Word into the world they understand so well. In reality, the impending confluence of waters is unavoidable, and staying the course without responding to change will steer the global church straight into a turbulent future. The greatest danger is that the valuable treasure carried by the church—the best news the world can ever hear—will be risked because leaders lack the stomach, mind, or heart to engage the changing times.

The ancient prophet Isaiah spoke to just this kind of challenge when he said,

> *Thus says the LORD, who makes a way in the sea, a path in the mighty waters, who brings out chariot and horse, army and warrior; they lie down, they cannot rise, they are extinguished, quenched like a wick: Do not remember the former things, or consider the things of old. I am about to do a new thing; now it springs forth, do you not perceive it? (Isa. 43:16–19 NRSV)*

CHAPTER 1

The 7 Global Currents

All Bets Are Off

"The expectations are unreasonable! I am but one small pastor in a tiny church in Africa, but the challenges are getting greater and greater!" the Kenyan pastor vented during a tea break at a leadership conference in East Africa.

As a pastor's kid, I thought I recognized those post-sermon insecurities and doubts. They had been my father's constant carp. Today, friends of mine who are pastors admit to being tormented by the very same gremlins. But this was not a case of my father's sermon angst.

"You see," the pastor continued, "what has happened is that quite a few of my parishioners have told me that they prefer the sermons of the televangelist whom they watch on TV before church every Sunday. Perhaps you have heard of the fellow, he's an American … T. D. Jakes?"

"Oh my," I said. Of course I knew of Jakes, who graced the cover of *Time* magazine in 2001 with the title "Is This Man the Next Billy Graham?" Jakes is a Dallas-based, African-American pastor who draws 30,000 worshipers to his church, has written several best-seller books, is pastor to the Dallas Cowboys and other celebrities, and runs anti-poverty programs in both Dallas and Kenya. He preached at a private church service for President-elect Obama on the morning of his inauguration and has prayed with the President on numerous phone calls.

That Kenyan pastor, who lacked formal training, a library, an assistant, or compensation, had pushed himself to work harder and harder to deliver sermons that were biblically truthful and culturally relevant. Suddenly, though, he found himself in a classic twenty-first-century bind. He was a Kenyan ministering to Kenyans in Kenya, but he had been unwittingly thrust into a global, cross-cultural dilemma. He had not gone to another country as a missionary. Rather, another country (America, in this case) had come into his church—and his church would never be the same. America was not the problem: His parishioners could just as easily tune in to televised preachers from South Korea, Australia, or Germany.

The challenge facing the pastor was that global media seamlessly and invisibly infiltrated his Kenyan culture. Further, I believe that this "cultural creep" is not the exception, but rather the rule in most countries around the world.[1]

As I met more leaders like my Kenyan friend, I grew increasingly curious to know just which trends were on the loose, in which countries, and what changes they were causing. The answers were important to me as a foundation executive, as I directed grants around the world, but I felt that something much bigger was also at stake: whether the global church could unlearn old irrelevancies and learn new realities as it steered into the next era.

A mission scholar said, "If you really want to understand the future of Christianity, go and see what is happening in Asia, Africa, Latin America … that's where the action is."[2] So, my colleagues and I decided to do just that. Between June 2006 and June 2007, we conducted 151 one-hour interviews with church leaders in nineteen countries. We called it the Global Church Listening Tour.

We interviewed indigenous seminarians, pastors, missionaries, and laypeople. We met them in churches, offices, schools, restaurants, tea shops, hotel rooms, trains, planes, cars, and boats throughout Asia, Africa, and Latin America. We asked all interviewees the following fifteen questions and transcribed their answers—about the state of the indigenous church in their country; the impact and effectiveness of Western missionaries and aid workers in their country; and the ways in which globalization is affecting local ministry in their country.

- With which denomination or church are you most closely affiliated?
- What are the three most urgent needs of the church in your country?
- What is the state of the church in your country?
- What are your dreams for the church in your country?
- What are the greatest strengths and weaknesses of people in your country, not just Christians?
- Which of the following are appropriate ways for the Western church to support the church in your country: short-term missions? Money? Evangelism? Church planting? Leadership development? Humanitarian aid?
- Describe the good and bad effects of missionaries in your country.
- Which country has sent the most missionaries to your country?
- What would you wish for foreign missionaries to know about your culture and society?
- As an American, I am curious to know what you think are the best and worst personal characteristics of American missionaries.
- Has the nature of relationships between foreign missionaries and local Christians changed in the past ten years?
- How are younger Christians different than their parents, and do they practice their faith differently?
- How has your country changed, for better or worse, in terms of culture, economics, politics, and religion because of other countries' influence?
- Are there ministry approaches that are no longer as effective as they used to be because of changing times?
- Which countries have affected your country the most?

In conducting the Listening Tour, my colleagues and I consistently met with a telling response—surprise that Americans would travel to poorer countries, ask questions, and listen. An American foundation with large amounts of money seeking the insights of indigenous church leaders in the developing world? At first, this caused suspicion, but ultimately it spread profound encouragement.

Deeply appreciative of being asked, the survey participants were remarkably forthcoming and thoughtful. I felt honored as they shared with me their indigenous perspectives, reminding me of long-simmering issues and also opening my eyes to new on-the-ground realities.

As the Listening Tour data came in, seven prevalent trends began to emerge. These 7 Global Currents flow invisibly and powerfully, under and around the global church. As identified in the Listening Tour, they are:

1. **Mercy:** Social justice has become a global imperative, especially among youth and young adults. For Christians, this will lead to an increasing emphasis on meeting physical needs in addition to continuing the long-standing emphasis on evangelism.

2. **Mutuality:** Leaders from traditionally poor countries increasingly have education, access, technology, and growing economies … and they will demand to be heard. Global church leaders from traditionally powerful countries will need to account for these new perspectives and voices.

3. **Migration:** Relocation among nations and regions is on the rise and will be rampant—especially to cities—whether for jobs, war, schooling, tourism, or politics. All future Christian outreaches will need to adapt their message for radically diverse audiences.

4. **Monoculture:** The cultures of all countries will become more and more similar, thanks to the spread of worldwide images, ideals,

celebrities, and ad campaigns. Christians seeking to communicate with global neighbors will need to be aware that marketing from outside their borders now shapes many of their deepest values.

5. **Machines:** Cell phones, GPS, television, and the Internet are transforming lifestyles worldwide. The future global church must recognize how newfound abilities to communicate, travel, and consume are changing individuals' lives and values, too.

6. **Mediation:** While there is much talk of the world's flattening, partisan rifts are actually proliferating. Splinter groups now have more communication avenues for inciting discord and attracting sympathizers than ever, and the global church must find a mediating role amid increasing polarization of all kinds.

7. **Memory:** Even as globalization reshapes the world, every nation and region has distinct histories that have profoundly shaped their society. Visitors must understand how yesterday affects today, in ways potentially undermining because they are invisible and unstated.

These Currents do not respect national or ethnic boundaries. Their invisibility makes them doubly potent, because they are relentless and dominant—but often overlooked. These Currents will powerfully alter the global church's future direction—for good or evil—depending on how quickly and wisely the church reacts.

My job as executive director of a private foundation has afforded me an enviable string of private tutoring sessions from great leaders in the global church. One day I might meet with a publisher from Moscow, the next day a politician from Sierra Leone, and then a substance-abuse counselor from

Mexico, a summer camp director from Romania, a seminary president from Egypt, a researcher from China, and a church planter from Ghana. I have also met American ministry greats: the urban ministry leader from Pasadena, the megachurch pastor from Manhattan, the substance-abuse counselor from Richmond, and the missions expert from Berkeley. It has all been part of the job.

My tutors come from more than one hundred nations, and not just the powerful ones. Although incredibly diverse, these men and women are consistent in how they describe their societies back home as modernizing and changing, rendering old stereotypes counterproductive. They do not characterize any single Global Current as totally negative or positive, but recognize that each of them could be harnessed for good or ill. The Currents are reliable tools for those who would help lead the global church into a bold and relevant future—to skate to where the puck is going to be.

I have been asked why today's followers of Christ—in New Delhi or Lima or Sydney—should care about the 7 Global Currents. My best answer is that the Currents will help people to reconcile their faith with their world—to connect Sundays with the rest of the week and provide a perspective on religion's centrality in the world today. The church's mission is to represent Jesus Christ to the people of the world, and I believe that the Currents will help the church understand what those people are like and how they are changing.

The practice of watching the changing world and constantly adjusting approaches accordingly is second nature in so many fields, but not in the worldwide Christian church.[3] Mission practitioners and scholars have traditionally focused on specific people, cultures, or countries—a noble undertaking as missionaries engaged with distant, remote locations that had seen few outsiders and where there was little or no written record.

But global church leaders today can no longer merely be specialists; they must also be generalists. In an age when trends spread "virally," significant events in the military, academic, media, economic, marketing, and financial worlds have profound impact on the global church's efforts. One global church scholar notes that "there used to be a global community of binary culture brokers: people who understood American culture and Singaporean culture from extensive, direct experience. Now there is an expanding global community of global culture brokers: people who understand many cultures from extensive, direct experience."[4] In the future, global church experts and practitioners must learn to navigate the 7 Global Currents in our all-bets-are-off world.

Just what do I mean by an *all-bets-are-off world?* Even in the most provincial or remote venue, global forces are now at play. Nothing seems to remain the same from year to year, week to week. Change is the norm. Once again, rivers provide a helpful metaphor. In a classic passage, American author Mark Twain describes the harrowing task of piloting riverboats on the Mississippi River over the course of days, seasons, and years when seemingly nothing remains the same. As I reflected on the challenge of adjusting to changing mission environments in the globalizing world, I thought back to Twain's wonderful description:

> One cannot easily realize what a tremendous thing it is to know every detail of twelve hundred miles of river and know it with absolute exactness. If you will take the longest street in New York, and travel up and down it, conning its features patiently until you know every house and window and lamppost and big and little sign by heart ... [a]nd then, if you will go on until you know every street–crossing, the character, size, and position of the crossing-stones.... Next, if you will take half of the signs in that long street, and change their places once a month, and still manage to know their new positions accurately

on dark nights, and keep up with these repeated
changes without making any mistakes, you will
understand what is required of a pilot's peerless
memory by the fickle Mississippi.[5]

That is the kind of environment in which the Christian church finds
itself today. Global trends and tools are being unleashed in one part of
the globe and immediately transforming local environments half a world
away—from Dallas to Nairobi and back again. As unfair or difficult as it
may be, my Kenyan friend must now consider and harness the influence of
television broadcasting and other forms of media from countries all around
the world. No longer may he merely remove himself to a quiet place,
immerse himself in the Bible, and emerge with a word for his flock. Now,
he must also take into account what is happening around the world—
including T. D. Jakes' latest sermon playing every Sunday before church.
And Jakes, too, as his parishioners grow more eager to serve the needs of
others around the globe, must stay tuned to the cries of people as far away
from Dallas as Kenya and Kampala and Kabul.

Thomas Friedman writes, "Today, more than ever, the traditional
boundaries between politics, culture, technology, finance, national security,
and ecology are disappearing. You often cannot explain one without referring to the others, and you cannot explain the whole without reference to
them all."[6] This practice, which Friedman calls "information arbitrage,"[7] is
just what the global church needs today, and the 7 Global Currents are just
the right tool.

But take heart. The task is an interesting one—quite fun, actually.
The happy result will be that the global church's efforts will be built upon
a current, relevant, and indigenous base. For Christians seeking to be faithful and relevant in the changing world, the 7 Currents offer new ways to
pray, think, give, send, and go. Most strategically, the Currents provide a
starter kit for a new generation of globally minded Christians who want

to see God's kingdom come—in brothels and barrios, in statehouses and criminal courts, in movie theaters and boardrooms, and in rain forests and greenbelts.

CHAPTER 2

Mercy

The Gospel as Yoke

His words were terse: "Put away your cell phone and take the battery out too." My host was obviously not pleased. My cell phone had rung as soon as he picked me up at the airport for our ride along the border. He seemed to have no patience for self-obsessed Americans with little sense for security or discretion. I was baffled as to why I needed to take my battery out, but I dared not ask. Someone else in our car later explained that "listeners" could tap into our turned-off cell phones and monitor our location and even our conversation as long as the batteries were in place.

As our car sped through the jet-black night, I was transfixed by the hills looming on the other side of the river. Not a single light twinkled, because electricity was severely limited there … and because the government prohibited residents along such a sensitive border. The landscape was unremarkable on its face, but what else could I expect from "The Hermit Kingdom"?

I had known this trip would involve stress and intrigue. The week before, in relatively "open" China, I had experienced small security wake-up calls. In a Beijing hotel hallway, an underground church leader went mute in mid-conversation, motioned to a tiny ceiling-mounted camera aimed our way, and nudged me toward the privacy of my nearby room. But North Korea, ominously dark across the river, promised to be far more oppressive than anything I had ever experienced.

The Tumen River forms the border for several hundred miles between China's northeast Manchuria region and North Korea. Shallow and narrow, it is a favored crossing point for North Korean refugees defecting across the Chinese border. Armed guards of the Democratic People's Republic of Korea (DPRK) heavily patrol the border with orders to shoot anyone sneaking across either way.[1] The area I was visiting was all the more sensitive because it was just a few miles from Russia. How sobering, when we drove over a hill in China the next morning, to see the Russian border a few hundred yards to the north and North Korea a few hundred yards across the river to the east! That put me on edge.

My host that week operates a Christian ministry that provides humanitarian relief to North Koreans. What he told me those days both challenged my imagination and pierced my heart.

Located on the same latitude as Scotland, Scandinavia, and Alaska, North Korea is dark and cold much of the year. The area is under snow for months on end during the winter, and the Tumen River freezes solid. My host told me how most winter mornings, standing on the China side of the frozen river, he sees fresh tracks in the snow from people who had trudged back and forth during the previous night. He explained that during the long winter nights when guards and all others burrow indoors, relief efforts into North Korea move into high gear.

Who, I wondered, would trudge during freezing nights through snowdrifts across icy rivers, illegally crossing the border *into* the most repressive regime on the face of the earth? This country has topped the "World Watch List" for seven years as the very worst country for persecution of Christians.[2] Who would choose to enter North Korea, where people routinely disappear into prison camps, suffering interrogation, persecution, torture, or death, never to be heard from again? At the beginning of the twenty-first century, many viewed North Korea as the world's most barbaric practitioner of democide, "governments' intentional killing—whether by induced famine, or forced labor, assassinations, extrajudicial executions, massacres, to full-scale genocide—of civilians."[3] It is completely understandable that there would be a mass of one-way footprints heading *out of* North Korea toward relative freedom in China … but who would cross that river and risk their lives to go *in?*

The global church, that's who, as it practices compassion and aid for desperate and forgotten people around the world. What's more, footprints pointing straight into the face of danger and despair are replicated hourly around the world wherever people have dire needs of any kind. This is not a new development, for Christians have long answered their calling to serve the needs of others. Now, though, the opportunities for relief assistance are greater than ever, as natural and man-made crises are creating unprecedented misery and loss on the global stage—and as technology allows people at a distance to learn about the crises and travel swiftly to help.

Just as a rash of global natural crises is occurring around the world, there has also arrived a new generation of students and young adults who view service to others as a defining expression of their faith. Twentieth-century author Frederick Buechner wrote, "The place God calls you to is the place where your deep gladness and the world's deep hunger meet."[4] As it intersects with this generation of students and young adults, the global church must model Jesus Christ, whose words survive today *precisely* because they were accompanied by acts of service and sacrifice.

Humanitarian needs figured prominently in the Global Church Listening Tour. In India, one third of interviewees responded that the church's strongest future role would be providing Mercy, in the form of education, outreach to lower castes, health care, literacy programs, and ministry to women. Likewise, Latin American interviewees felt that the best way for outside Christians to help in their country is through acts of Mercy.

In the coming years, respect and relevance will flow to the global church when it does what it was created to do: to fill gaping holes, both spiritual and physical, in the lives of unnoticed, unwanted people. This is the heart language of the next generation, non-Christians and Christians alike, and it is the first Global Current—*Mercy*.

When Mission Marm left the United States to serve overseas in the early 1970s, she was a typical player in twentieth-century missions. She left behind hopes of remaining connected with her home country and fully planned to spend decades in the field. More than thirty years later, as her successors disperse around the globe, they are a new breed of Christian worker impassioned by justice and Mercy. I call them the Mercy Generation.

It is human nature for older generations to underestimate the ability and readiness of younger people. We Christians, of course, are no different. During the Global Church Listening Tour, the middle-aged respondents consistently offered wary assessments of young adult Christians. A national mission leader in India told me, "They think differently in every aspect of life. They are more pro-small groups. They don't like big churches. They think ahead of us." This man who had been married for forty years to the woman his parents arranged for him also wryly noted, "They don't ask permission for marriage."

Younger Christians are often ambivalent about the institutional church,[5] but completely committed to Mercy. It is crucial for this Global Current to be understood, accepted, and harnessed by bunkhouse visitors on both sides of the generation gap. Apple Guy must see his vision and leadership accepted by the global church. And I believe that Mission Marm and older Christian leaders must welcome new movements and approaches.

The best way to share my excitement about the future global church is to introduce three remarkable young friends from three continents, who powerfully expanded my understanding of what faithfulness and fruitfulness look like today.

DEBBIE WALKER

Debbie Walker was raised in traditional, middle-class Dublin, Ireland. Children invariably find their distinct roles in families, and Debbie was always all about justice. Despite being the fifth of six children, she was never reluctant to express her opinions or take charge. "I was always getting in the middle," she laughingly recalls, "trying to straighten arguments out, saying, 'No, that's not fair.'" Her siblings believed Debbie was destined to be a lawyer.

Like so many of today's twentysomethings, Debbie grew up with global awareness and exposure unimaginable to preceding generations. Her young heart was indelibly pricked when she visited India and witnessed firsthand the subhuman, repressive treatment of women. Even at that age, she says, "I realized that it was women who needed to reach women in India. A man couldn't do it, because it was just not appropriate in a country like that."

Debbie was an excellent student in high school, strong enough to apply for a spot at Ireland's top universities. She did well on the state entrance exams and was admitted to study law at the very competitive University College in Dublin, the country's largest university and alma mater of James Joyce. She decided on law, not because of the career prospects it offered, but because she wanted expertise in advocating justice for the poor. At University College, she mostly took courses on international law. After graduating, she spent a year sitting for eight exams in the Law Society in Dublin; her career was definitely moving ahead.

"I began the process of applying for jobs with Dublin law firms, but after a grueling year of exams I just wanted to get away," Debbie recalls. "India was always a special place for me, so I decided to spend a few weeks visiting my sister who lived there." That was in the fall of 2006.

I saw Debbie three and a half years later. She was still in India, with no plans to return to that law job. Instead, Debbie has spent the last several years working for a young, growing Christian organization called Freedom Firm. She lives with, works with, and advocates for girls rescued from brothels in Pune and other cities in the state of Maharashtra. "Our approach is to identify women in forced prostitution, assist the legal system in prosecution of the brothel owners and other perpetrators, help to mobilize law enforcement agencies to rescue the victims, and then provide those women with physical, emotional, social, and spiritual rehabilitation," she told me. "We work very closely with local governments, for without the government's involvement the perpetrators will simply regroup and resume. Freedom Firm has rescued ninety girls, and the legal team is working on dozens of additional criminal cases against perpetrators."

Debbie and the Mercy Generation represent a sea change for the global church. They are especially dedicated to being agents of compassion, justice, and mercy toward the last and the least, pulling the global church into the world in new ways. That is not to say that their focus on justice and mercy is brand new, because Christian workers have always embraced "holistic" ministries (Christian outreach that seeks to meet both spiritual and physical needs) to some degree. What is new, though, is the *universal* emphasis on Mercy by an entire generation[6] of followers of Christ all around the world.

A willingness to take detours off the beaten career path—in Debbie's case, choosing Freedom Firm over a law firm—is one of the defining characteristics of the Mercy Generation. From a spiritual perspective, they are heeding God's still, small voice. Young followers of Christ are motivated not by a traditional career sequence, but by a burning sense of urgency about the needs of the world.[7]

Another feature of the Mercy Generation is the attraction toward things new and small, as seen in Debbie's choice of a start-up ministry. Rather than the mega-organizations that characterized the ministry world in the second half of the twentieth century, this generation values locally-based, nimble solutions. That is why "social entrepreneurship" is the mantra now, both in Christian and secular organizations.

The *Stanford Social Innovation Review* is a case in point: Just one issue features four consecutive articles on wildly creative social entrepreneur programs addressing various global needs. None of these programs is Christian, but they are representative of the changing nonprofit sector in which the Mercy Generation operates. For instance, there is the story about Room to Read, which has opened five thousand libraries in Nepal in eight years and computer and language labs in Vietnam. Typical of the Mercy Generation's emphasis on environmental sustainability, Room to Read emphasizes reclaiming buildings, and four thousand of the libraries use existing local spaces. Another article describes ATREE, an Eastern Himalaya program that grows organic vegetables to supplement poor families' income. In the process, ATREE "protects fragile ecosystems, including the humans who rely on them." ATREE also conducts research on conservation and sustainable development and advocates for evidence-based environmental policy. Another organization, World of Good, connects artisans—mostly women in poor countries—with affluent, trendy consumers in the wealthy nations. Its Web site features an interactive introduction to fair trade, the philosophy that "producers in poor countries, whether they grow coffee or sew caftans, should receive just compensation from consumers in rich countries." Finally, there is an article on Grassroot Soccer, a program that uses local soccer stars in soccer-obsessed Africa to lead children through twenty hours of educational and trust-building activities dealing with HIV/AIDS. In a 2006 survey of Grassroot Soccer participants in Botswana, 90 percent had educated at least one person about HIV/AIDS, and the average participant went on to talk with three or more people about the disease.[8]

A defining characteristic of the Mercy Generation, and a departure from previous approaches that were strictly proclamation oriented, is what

I call an "evangelism too" approach. The Mercy Generation seeks to serve Jesus by doing justice and helping the poor … and proclaiming the gospel *too*. They serve others not just to convert them, but *because* they themselves have been converted.[9] As a case in point, Debbie's love for Christ and her commitment to justice drew her to a Christian organization that serves girls' physical and emotional needs while *also* ministering to their spiritual needs. That is the way the Mercy Generation lives out their faith.

Prominent New York pastor Tim Keller agrees, noting that "we live in a time when public esteem of the church is plummeting. For many outsiders or inquirers, the deeds of the church will be far more important than words in gaining plausibility. The leaders of most towns see 'word-only' churches as costs to their community, not a value. Effective churches will be so involved in deeds of mercy and justice that outsiders will say, 'we cannot do without churches like this.'"[10]

Gary Haugen is the founder of the International Justice Mission—a ministry with unique influence in challenging and shaping Christians in the Mercy Generation—and he sees younger followers of Christ helpfully pointing the global church beyond false distinctions: "It makes no sense as an authentic follower of Jesus to bifurcate those things…. If you don't care anything about the spiritual health of the people you are helping, then that is not truly, deeply loving them. But if you are attending to their spiritual needs without attending to the man beaten along the side of the road, that's not love either."[11]

Perhaps the overriding feature of the Mercy Generation is its comfort with ambiguity and contradiction, which is quite unlike the generation that preceded it. The book *unChristian* notes, "Young people engage in a nearly constant search for fresh experiences and new sources of motivation. They want to try things themselves…. If something doesn't work for them, or if they are not permitted to participate in the process, they quickly move on to something that grabs them…. They view life in a nonlinear, chaotic way, which means they don't mind contradiction and ambiguity."[12]

Clear as mud, right? Well, we should all get used to it, because the Mercy Generation is not a linear generation. The information they are incessantly bombarded with (through the Internet, cable television, text messages, Twitter, advertisements, and more) often comes without context or narrative, sometimes without a clear source. The people of this generation do not expect permanency, knowing that they are statistically likely to have three careers and change jobs every three-to-five years during their lifetimes.[13] They care about the entire world, knowing that they can go far away and return any time they need to; ubiquitous short-term mission trips foster perceptions of international Christian ministry as an experience, not a final destination. Young followers of Christ, therefore, are much more likely than their predecessors to do full-time Christian work for a season, but not for their whole lives. One of the best descriptions I have heard of this generation is that their lives look more like a disjointed episode of *Seinfeld* than the start-to-finish *Cosby Show*.[14]

The Mercy Generation also has a thoroughly new view on geography and place. They know that they can be active participants in worldwide movements without permanently relocating. Debbie Walker will feel that she is fully pursuing her calling whether she sits behind a desk in Dublin, Ireland, or raises holy hell in Pune, India. Even when she is serving Christ in the slums of Pune, she remains in virtual community with fellow believers back home. And her decision to go or stay is never permanent.

So will Debbie Walker ever return to practicing law? While talking on Skype one night, she gave me a classic Mercy Generation response: "I may practice law for a while, but I am not necessarily looking at one long, coherent career path. I simply know that whatever I do, I want to work with victims, help them in their healing process, and empower and equip them."

Especially if the preceding generations can manage to flex with them, Debbie and her generation will be an invaluable resource in a global church too often calcified, marginalized, and paralyzed at the Meeting of the Waters.

For her part, Debbie told me that she expects nothing less than tackling new challenges: "Healing and empowerment require women to go the distance."

ALLAN

I first met Allan over a meal in Richmond. He was on his way to a five-year program that would train him to live and serve God in countries that are lonely and hostile for Christians. We talked about his parents and their very conservative church back home in California. He had not finished college but was intellectually curious and an avid reader, and he had big designs for how he wanted to serve God. Allan was California-breezy and a little naive; like Apple Guy, his ideas and dreams had not been blunted by the realities of foreign Christian work. I hoped to keep up with him, but sort of doubted that would be possible.

A few years later, I made a site visit to a training center in a mission compound nestled in the mountains of Brazil. There, one hundred thirty young adults (including just two Americans) were engaged in intensive study of Scripture, spiritual formation, missiology, theology, apologetics, ethnology, and language—all pointing toward their particular country of focus. Because many of these young men and women would be sent to countries with very limited religious freedom, the project was steeped in security and secrecy. So sensitive is the program, in fact, that I have omitted descriptive facts that might compromise identities or divulge exact locations.

I had actually forgotten that Allan was in the program, so I was delighted to see him when I arrived at the compound. Allan and all of the men in the program had grown long, full beards, and all students wore peasant clothes to approximate the conditions in which they would soon find themselves. No student had his or her own money, but drew ten dollars each month from a common fund. The small dorm room I visited was crammed with six bunk beds, foot lockers, and just a six-foot-square patch of floor in the center of the room. It was a perfect laboratory for learning about servant leadership, humility, team building, and—naturally—conflict resolution. There was a heavy emphasis on building relationships of trust and accountability to prepare graduates to be sent out in teams after their three years of study.

After touring the grounds and meeting with students and administrators, I had to leave for the airport, and Allan volunteered to accompany me on the long ride. I was delighted for the conversation, partly to take my mind off our driver as he hand braked and skidded through a hundred switchbacks. The Brazilian driver helpfully pointed out several car wrecks as we sped by, saying, "Curva." I was relieved he knew curves could cause collisions.

Allan and I talked about books we had read and authors we liked, from classic theologians to modern cultural critics. When I mentioned I had read a recent controversial book by Christian author Brian McLaren, Allan shot forward in his seat: "Dude—I just read that book, and it is awesome! Dude, that is way cool!" He actually talked that way. As I saw Allan grinning, with his beard and floppy surfer hair, I thought to myself that you can take the guy out of California, but you can't take California out of the guy. I asked Allan if he had discussed the book with his pastor back home. "No way, dude!" he said. "He'd freak."

Allan and I discussed his calling to a ministry of service and compassion toward the poor. As a member of the Mercy Generation, he felt called first to comfort and then to convert, first to serve and then to save. He expressed his concern about global warming and globalization, and he said he hates abortion. But, typical of his generation, Allan was not an easy guy to peg. I found his range of perspectives to be unpredictable and invigorating.

Young men and women of the Mercy Generation are often quite grounded and radically devoted in their faith. However, the Mercy Generation does not view the gospel's good news as just a tool for evangelizing non-Christians; neither a carrot nor a stick, the gospel is their yoke to a world of needy people loved by God.

Not lacking in biblical convictions, the Mercy Generation may actually hold strong Christian viewpoints on *more* issues than did Mission Marm, which is not surprising since they have been exposed to infinitely more information than their parents or grandparents ever were. For instance, the Mercy Generation does care deeply about their parents' core Christian priorities like evangelism and discipleship, personal piety and Scripture study. But their "evangelism too" list goes further, including no-compromise moral issues like the environment, fair trade, sustainability, community, and global justice.

The Mercy Generation also has a fearless, risk-taking edge to it. Allan works in a place where the threat of violence is constant and Christians are unwelcome. This is certainly not new to this generation, but it is more pronounced in today's fractious world.

I recently had a phone conversation with Allan while he was in the States visiting family. For the past few years he has served a mountaineering program in a beautiful Muslim country that is hostile to stereotypical Christianity. With only a handful of indigenous Christians and very limited religious freedom for nationals or visitors, it is a place where conversion can cause job loss, persecution, or even imprisonment for nationals, and expatriates who evangelize are swiftly deported.

I cannot think of anyone better to bring a Christian witness into that country than my Mercy Generation friend with his contagious and wide-open love for people, his deep personal relationship with Christ, and his years of intensive training.

As usual, my conversation with Allan was random and delightful. He told me, "We want our business to be completely self-sufficient and to employ nationals, with us foreigners living very simple lives among the local people. That way, there's no fuzziness about our integrity or motives. In the old days, man, missionaries often worked from 'platforms,' shabby businesses that allowed them to stay in the country and evangelize. But that model of missionaries going over to other countries—without jobs that

really contributed to society—and never integrating into the culture …
dude, that model doesn't work, at least not in my country."

Allan continued, "In my country, every move we make is watched by
everyone—our fellow employees, our neighbors, and especially the government. I want to come into their country and straight up bless those people
by walking and sharing with them. And the whole time, yeah, for sure we're
reflecting Jesus. When we can, we talk about Him too."

When I think of Allan, I love the thought of him leading treks in
one of the most majestic mountain ranges in the world. He has learned
the local language, and I love to think about how "dude," "awesome," and
"whatever" translate into Arabic!

JOSEPH VIJAYAM

Joseph Vijayam is from Hyderabad, India, the only son in a prominent
Indian Christian family in a country where only 2 percent of the people
are Christians.[15] His grandfather, one of the first Anglican bishops in
India, was revered throughout the country. His father, a geology professor at India's largest university, was named Scientist of the Year by India's
government—at the same time as he was starting and running a major
parachurch ministry.

For most of his childhood, in a family well-known for its strong
Christian faith and service, Joseph felt like the black sheep. At home and
with his friends, he was rebellious. Early on, though, he learned that strong
academic performance earned him latitude in other areas of his life that
were not so exemplary. At St. George's Grammar School, Joseph was a top
student and "chief prefect." He always gravitated toward mathematics.

Right after high school Joseph took his first computer course.
Hyderabad, on the verge of becoming a leading global city in information
technology (IT), only had four computer institutes at the time. Today there
are thousands of them. Like many bright children of Indian leaders, Joseph

went to the United States to pursue his education, and he decided to study computer science. Around that time, he also embraced his parents' love of Christ as his own.

I first met Joseph in 2001 in Hyderabad, and it seems that we have reconnected every few years since—when he visited my office in Richmond, at a conference in Thailand, and then at his U.S. office in Colorado Springs. He has always struck me as thoughtful, purposeful, and gentle.

Joseph's background is extremely traditional, and so is his preppy wardrobe of khakis, button-down shirts, and loafers. His glasses are the kind that accountants wear, not the hip, black-rimmed ones of marketing- or media-types. He looks nothing like Debbie or Allan, but then again nothing about their generation is one-size-fits-all.

It was during his undergraduate years in California and subsequent MBA studies in Georgia that Joseph began to experience the generational pull toward Mercy. For him, his "evangelism too" dream was to combine technology, business, and ministry in an emerging field called "business as mission"(BAM).

"I did not want to be like so many students from poorer countries who pursue higher education in the United States and end up staying for the money and comfort. I had always vowed that I would fly back to India on the very same day as I took my last MBA exam in the U.S., and that's what I did, with my wife and our baby." This was not just national loyalty, but Joseph's Christian calling to a people and place.

That was more than a decade ago, and ever since, Joseph has consistently placed a high value on community, relationships, and fellowship. One major commonality of all members of the Mercy Generation is their zeal for community. Joseph and his Christian peers are committed to acts of Mercy, and they believe that those acts flow most naturally and efficiently from strong communities.

Upon returning to Hyderabad in 1996, Joseph began Olive Technology. "My company," he said, "is designed to be one hundred percent business and one hundred percent ministry. Our mission statement is a vivid example of BAM: Olive exists to provide human, technological, and financial resources to grow God's kingdom in India and worldwide."

Olive now employs eighty people. I asked Joseph how a profit-driven, competitive computer company could exemplify Mercy. The topic clearly energized Joseph, because I could barely write down his examples as quickly as he rattled them off.

"Most obviously," he said, "Olive releases other employees and me to do Christian ministry in India and abroad. Olive pays for travel and other needs incurred by employees who travel for ministry purposes. One Olive employee has started a church specifically for technology people in Hyderabad.

"Olive launched two Web sites, www.mahalife.com for pre-evangelism of non-Christians and www.mahajesus.com for discipleship of Christians.

"At Olive we take every possible opportunity to bring people closer to truth. We have voluntary daily devotionals and, although about seventy-five percent of Olive's employees are non-Christians, several of them attend. We host programs on Republic Day, Independence Day, Christmas, Easter, and more. On Valentine's Day, Olive invited other tech companies to a program called "Reality Check on Romantic Relationships," and four hundred people attended. The invitation carries much more weight when coming from another tech company instead of a Christian ministry. Next year, we hope to have a thousand people at the event.

"We really try to support Christian ministries in Hyderabad and throughout India. We provide free Web hosting for sixty Christian ministries. Olive makes financial giving to Christian ministries a top priority and a consistent practice."

As it relentlessly takes risks, the Mercy Generation encounters many impediments: public disapproval, friends' confusion, untested financial models, uncertain future paths, and even physical danger. Joseph acknowledged to me that Olive had to sacrifice higher profits by diverting money into ministry. "Olive hasn't grown the way a typical IT company does, especially one that has been in business for twelve years. Most of those companies, if they're still around, have gone through initial public offerings and have grown ten times, so there *is* a cost."

Debbie Walker continues to put off her law career as she chases her calling in India. Allan lives under the threat of harassment or detention by government security in his country while facing skepticism among Christians about the effectiveness of his "evangelism too" efforts. Debbie, Allan, and Joseph have all counted the costs of innovation, of sharing the yoke with Jesus.

Joseph was also quick to point out to me that the Mercy Generation is not restricted to Christians. "After an earthquake in 1993 when thirty-five thousand people died, India was entirely reliant on foreign funding. When the tsunami hit in 2004, the Indian government told the world that we did not need funding from outside. Software companies and call centers raised 18 million dollars within a couple of days. Almost the next day after the tsunami, twenty Olive employees asked for time off to go to the tsunami-affected areas with blankets, food, and money. And this trend isn't unique to Christian believers—it's the younger generation around the world. In India, younger people are in workplaces where they interact with people from the United States, and they see your belief that all men are created equal. Then the upper-class IT Indians begin to treat lower-caste Indians that way. Spreading values through commerce just happens naturally, which is one reason why BAM is so powerful."

Three generations of Vijayam men portray the evolution of ministry in the marketplace. "My grandfather the Bishop and my father the professor shared a common approach," Joseph noted, "separating ministry from the workplace. My grandfather's ministry was all in the church. My father's ministry was also outside of his job, as he poured himself into parachurch organizations. But now, Olive Tech and hundreds of other 'kingdom companies' around the world are the logical next step in this progression: the merging of business and ministry."

Mercy: mercy in emancipating, mercy in mountaineering, mercy in the marketplace—and yes, mercy in ministry. The concept can be perplexing to Christians with dualistic views of vocation and ministry as fundamentally separate. But the Mercy Generation leans away from "either/or" toward "both/and" solutions. Debbie, Allan, and Joseph have all taken innovative steps to reshape their worlds so that their passions merge: for Debbie it's law and justice, for Allan it's mountaineering and discipleship, and for Joseph it's business and ministry.

Mercy Currents are breaking out all over the global church among young and old believers alike. I think back to the Tumen River, which runs between China and North Korea.

Ministry work in North Korea today must begin with Mercy—food, clothing, rescue, and money—for two reasons. First, the physical needs are so raw, pervasive, and obvious that it is unthinkable to ignore them. North Korea has been beset by starvation since the mid-1990s, when a famine racked the country. The famine's toll reached more than 2.5 million casualties,[16] and today more than a fourth of the population suffers from malnutrition or hunger.[17]

Second, while there is obviously a need for evangelism, the official barriers to it are monumental. North Korea is the world's most ruthless country in suppressing and punishing religious expression of any sort, except worship of leader Kim Jong Il and his deceased father and national founder, Kim Il Sung.

Only eighty thousand of the nation's 23 million citizens, an astonishingly low .003 percent, are estimated to be Christians.[18] China, where conservative estimates peg 7.25 percent of the 1.3 billion people as Christian, seems free in comparison. Courageous Chinese Christians are also doing extraordinary ministry work in North Korea. Some offer safe houses for smuggled escapees; some store and send food and supplies into North Korea; others train Christian workers who will go into North Korea; still others smuggle Bibles.

One of them, "Katie," is still emblazoned in my memory. I met her at a safe house in northeast China, not far from the border with North Korea. There she received shelter, medical attention, spiritual mentoring, and counseling between her daring trips into North Korea. My encounter with her was riveting.

On a cold, harsh day when the wind whipped across the barren landscape, I was surprised when Katie arrived at our meeting place in a plum suit, glass dangle earrings, and pearls. Sitting ramrod straight, she spoke through a translator, recounting endless details as two hours flew by. Several times she also fought back tears when recalling the constant danger, stress, and oppression.

"I was raised by an aunt in Yanji, the closest Chinese city to North Korea," she said. "Like many Chinese in the Yanji-Tumen region, I did not like North Koreans. They are not beasts, but they live like it. They curse, fight, steal, yell, hate. North Korea today is like I have read Communist China used to be."

Yet, even as she had a deep aversion to North Koreans, she felt inexplicably drawn toward serving them. For five years, she shuttled in and out of North Korea. She purchased a corn noodle machine, in a small example of business as mission, and took it to villages where she sold food to starving North Koreans. "I didn't just sell them food," she said, "but I would occasionally cook a pig and serve an entire village, to bring measures of joy and fellowship into their sad lives."

At the same time, she was consistently finding ways to do something mortally dangerous—telling North Korean villagers about the gospel of Jesus Christ. She was pursuing her Mercy venture wholeheartedly, and she was also wholehearted in sharing with North Korean friends why in the world she voluntarily came to their villages.

I own a copy of one of the Bibles that Katie smuggled, a tiny-print version about the size and thickness of a book of matches. She buried the Bibles in the ground in North Korea to avoid the risk of carrying them on her person or putting a North Korean at risk by leaving it with them. North Koreans caught with Bibles are sent to prison camps along with their entire families. Some estimates say that as many as a quarter of all North Koreans are currently in prison.[19]

Katie's efforts bore much fruit as twenty families turned in faith to Jesus Christ. Too much fruit, some might say, as North Korean security police caught wind of Katie. They captured all of the converts and jailed one of them, then confronted Katie with transcripts and a complete record of every sermon she had privately taught to individuals or small groups.

"The government was harsh," Katie continued, "and they interrogated me every day for five weeks, fifteen hours a day. I knew I might be killed for activities that threatened the government, but I felt the presence of the Lord and laughed at the interrogator, for he was a paper tiger.

"A higher-ranking provincial official heard about me and traveled to interrogate me. I witnessed to him. He asked me, 'Do you know who I am? You must be crazy!' I told him, 'No, I am wise.' He asked me, 'Who is behind you—the United States or South Korea?' and I answered, 'Only my God.' The official interrogated me day after day, but then he also began to bring me food because I was losing my health."

Katie's voice quickened, her eyes fixed on some distant point, and her words spilled out in excitement. "On the night before my sentence would be handed down, I went to bed filled with gladness. I was certain I would be executed on the next day, and I was overjoyed to think of being lined up with other martyrs. I knew God would be so pleased. I would be dying in happiness."

Her story played out differently, of course. Instead of execution, she was released with grave official warnings. The Public Security Bureau drove her to the border at the Tumen River, where they pointed her toward

China. They allowed her to walk through customs and across the quarter-mile bridge to be reunited with her waiting husband and family in the country she loves, China.

That was several years ago, and I have not heard from her since. Having met her once, though, I know what her captors also surely know: Katie will be back in North Korea, because Mercy propels her.

MERCY
Representative Organizations

The Mercy Generation brings an "evangelism too" approach to Christian ministry, emphasizing mercy, justice, and evangelism *too*. This approach is not new, but its widespread adoption is. While ministries from the twentieth century more often emphasized proclamation, in recent years Mercy ministries have proliferated. Following is a list of seven young organizations, mostly nonprofits, which represent the Global Current of Mercy:

1. **Blessed Earth:** In 2006, Dr. Matthew Sleeth left his emergency-room practice, and he and his family cut their fossil fuel and electricity use by two thirds. He wrote *Serve God, Save the Planet* to advance the eco-evangelism movement. The Sleeths began Blessed Earth in 2006 to work with churches, colleges, and media to promote measurable environmental change and meaningful spiritual growth. (www.blessedearth.org)

2. **Blood:Water Mission:** Founded by the Grammy-Award-winning band Jars of Clay in 2005, Blood:Water Mission is a grassroots nonprofit with a goal of helping community leaders combat the HIV/AIDS and water crises in Africa. Only four years after its founding, Blood:Water Mission had installed over six hundred wells in eleven countries and trained almost 250,000 people in sanitation and hygiene. (www.bloodwatermission.com)

3. **HOPE International:** Since 1997, HOPE International has promoted microfinancing programs in developing countries such as Afghanistan, China, the Democratic Republic of Congo, the Dominican Republic, Haiti, India, Russia, and Rwanda. In 2008,

HOPE International employed over 250,000 nationals through microcredit programs, and saw a 99.6 percent repayment rate for its loans. (www.hopeinternational.org)

4. **International Justice Mission:** Founded by Gary Haugen in 1997, International Justice Mission (IJM) is a human rights organization that works with other countries' local justice systems to protect the rights of victims of violent oppression. IJM is present in Cambodia, the Philippines, Thailand, India, Kenya, Rwanda, Uganda, Zambia, Bolivia, Guatemala, Honduras, and Peru. (www.ijm.org)

5. **TOMS Shoes:** TOMS Shoes is a for-profit shoe company founded in 2006. For every pair of shoes that TOMS sells, it provides a pair of shoes to a child in need. TOMS gave away 140,000 pairs of shoes in 2007 and 2008 and projected giving another 300,000 in South America and Haiti in 2009. (www.tomsshoes.com)

6. **Viva Network:** Viva Network, founded in 1996, is a UK-based nonprofit working to connect projects helping at-risk children throughout North America, Latin America, India, Asia, Europe, and Africa. Viva's goal is to form a cohesive network of indigenous and international organizations in order to better the lives of kids. (www.viva.org)

7. **Invisible Children:** In 2003, three recently graduated American filmmakers traveled to northern Uganda in search of adventure; instead, they found child soldiers, millions of displaced people, and the passion to create Invisible Children. Invisible Children operates in the United States, Uganda, and the United Kingdom, running campaigns and a scholarship program. Its last campaign

raised over 17 million dollars to raise awareness and aid post-war reconstruction in northern Uganda. (www.invisiblechildren.com)

CHAPTER 3

Mutuality

Upside-Down Maps

One sermon in my prosperous suburban church changed my life. I have attended Third Presbyterian Church for more than twenty-five years, and I have been blessed there by a string of pastors with spiritual depth, knowledge, and experience. But none of those pastors were preaching on that particular Sunday. Instead, it was a visiting Indian preacher, barefoot and wearing a knee-length tunic.

Back then, my experience as an international traveler was mostly in modern, industrialized nations. Squirming in my church seat, I found myself uneasily wrestling with issues that were newly highlighted by his very presence. The affluence and homogeneity of my church. The fact that the visiting preacher seemed so highly educated, despite his peasant dress. The fact that he preached with confidence and even a hint of prophetic impatience … all while standing in front of my wealthy church in bare feet!

That was my first image of C. B. Samuel. Beginning that Sunday morning, and many times since, C. B. has profoundly challenged my understanding of what it means to be a follower of Christ.

I might have previously dismissed visiting speakers as mere curiosities, but that morning Rev. Samuel was an agent to my awakening. All of the "first glance" differences that were so obvious that morning—clothing, geography, language, wealth—were just the tip of the iceberg. Curiosity about clothes and accents emerged into more enlightened views on poverty, justice, mercy, illness, compassion, teamwork, humility, and servanthood.

A brilliant expositor and a very smart man, with university degrees in both mathematics and divinity, C. B. Samuel was a regular lecturer at the Oxford Centre for Mission Studies. What struck me most about the man, though, was his moral authority. He had spent fifteen years at the Evangelical Fellowship of India Commission on Relief (EFICOR), where he was the top man in the largest Christian organization serving the poorest people in India. I sensed that he was a humble man of great power: He could comfort the afflicted and afflict the comfortable.

You might wonder, as I did, about the bare feet. He said he was simply following Moses' example of shedding his sandals in order to demonstrate reverence for God and humility in his role as God's messenger.

What an ironic twist: We American churchgoers often dress up to gain approval from others, and this man dressed down to deflect honor to God. I felt convicted that the Indian man seemed to have depth and abundance in lasting matters, while I feared that my abundance was mostly in material things.

And then, another irony: I sat there wondering—worrying even—a little—about how he viewed us, me and my church. There I was, a relatively wealthy American, feeling intimidated by the small man in peasant garb whom my church supported. Even though I had been a follower of Christ all of my life, I knew I did not understand Christian life nearly as deeply as he. I possessed so much, but he did too, and I knew I needed more of what he had.

That was my first experience with the second Global Current—*Mutuality*.

I believe that Mutuality is needed wherever countries or people with ostensible power and wealth (that's me) interact with people ostensibly without (that's Rev. Samuel). With our brothers and sisters from developing nations, their outward appearances of poverty and subservience can hide deep reserves of spiritual, intellectual, and cultural wealth.

Viewing people without money or power as equals is not only the right choice—it is becoming the only choice. During the Global Church Listening Tour, almost every participant referred to changed relationships between foreign ministry workers and indigenous followers of Christ. They pointed to increasing partnership and less paternalistic control by outside missionaries or funding agencies toward local Christians.

For generations, outside Christians ably spearheaded evangelism and church-planting ministries in countries around the world. Now, however, indigenous Christians have been empowered by education, travel, and access, and they are confidently taking charge. For instance, we asked Listening Tour interviewees whether it was appropriate for outside missionaries to evangelize and plant churches in their country, and the responses were consistent:

- "No, evangelism is a strength of the Ecuadoran church."

- "No, outsiders should no longer be the primary evangelists to Africa."

- "Only if done with Ugandans."

- "No, enough Guatemalans are planting churches."

- "No, it's better for the Nepalese to do this."

- "Maybe if it's combined with a local church or group. But we need Brazilian leadership."

- "Indians should probably plant their own churches."

Along with increased confidence, some respondents also showed levels of resentment and indignation about past relationships. A very prominent African pastor pointed out that, not only is the need decreasing for outside missionaries *to* Africa, but wealthier countries now need missionaries *from* Africa to steer them away from increasingly materialistic and secular cultural leanings.

Mutuality may be the single most important Current for understanding how to support, work with, and pray for Christian movements around the world. Unfortunately, practicing Mutuality does not come easily to people of wealth, including this American. People with money and power easily become blind to resources that Christians from other countries bring to the table. True Mutuality among players from different corners of the globe is, in fact, quite rare. The urge to "go it alone" is powerful. Collaboration, and the Mutuality it fosters, is expensive in terms of time, energy, and money … and ego.

Fortunately, there are also several voices in the global church that are advocating Mutuality, including the influential Lausanne Movement.[1] In seeking to practice Mutuality with people from other backgrounds, Christians around the world must actively build relationships based on equality, reciprocity, interdependency, and accountability. The formerly poor and backward countries that are now global powers, or fast becoming so, will require nothing less.

Since that first draw to the need for Mutuality, I have seen again and again that believers from poorer nations understand humility before God and dependency on God in a deeper way than I could, largely because they have lived in countries where physical deprivation and humiliating dependency are commonplace. In comparison, my understanding of those issues is superficial or theoretical. I have learned that the world is filled with brothers and sisters like C. B. Samuel, from whom I have so much to learn.

Mutuality is not a concept that I came to understand while sitting in my office in Richmond, Virginia. For most of my life I have been like the proverbial fish that cannot describe water: I didn't know what I didn't know. As a white American Christian male, I assumed that *my* world was *the* world.

Breakthroughs in my understanding of the Global Currents have come at the strangest places and times. With Mutuality, another "aha" occurred during a two-day trip into a war zone with a Ugandan priest.

Rev. David Zac Niringiye is the assistant bishop of the Kampala Diocese in the Church of Uganda. He is one of his country's great Christian leaders, circulating not just in formal church circles but also in villages and slums. Wherever he goes, people address him as *mzee* (pronounced "muh-*zay*")—a Swahili word meaning an old man or elder who possesses great experience and, most of all, wisdom. Zac Niringiye is now *mzee* to me.

Widely recognized as a man of peace, Rev. Niringiye was appointed as chairman of the Northern Uganda Task Force for the Uganda Joint Christian Council (UJCC). For twenty years, messianic rebel Joseph Kony and his Lord's Resistance Army (LRA) gripped the nation with a campaign of terror in northern Uganda, killing more than twenty thousand people, abducting sixty thousand, and sending two million more fleeing from their homes toward the government's squalid "Internally Displaced Persons" (IDP) camps. A historic round of peace talks began on July 12, 2006, with a September 12 deadline imposed by Uganda's President Museveni. While I was in the capital city of Kampala that summer, people throughout Uganda and the world were closely following the cease-fire talks on radios, televisions, and newspapers, in hopes that good news might finally emerge from that troubled region. When I met him in July 2006, Rev. Niringiye had an important and visible national platform.

While statistics alone could never describe the LRA, they do help to portray its physical, psychological, spiritual, and economic toll in northern Uganda. In 2003, 74 percent of all households in northern Uganda were without a single blanket, compared with 25 percent nationally. Ninety-one percent of the houses were grass-thatched, compared with only 21 percent in western Uganda. Seventy percent of all children in the Gulu, Kitgum, and Pader regions of northern Uganda were considered "underweight or stunted." Amazingly, there were only 236 businesses in northern Uganda, compared with almost 102,000 in central Uganda. In 2004, HIV/AIDS accounted for 69 percent of all deaths in the Gulu region, fueled partly by "survival sex"—girls offering themselves in exchange for soap, food, or school fees.[2]

An entire generation of northern Ugandans numbly watched their villages demolished, harvests destroyed, houses burned, and relatives killed. Particularly heinous, the LRA's preferred recruitment method was to abduct children—very young children—from villages and schools, enlist them in the army, and teach them to kill, often beginning with their own families. The so-called LRA rebels, therefore, are actually children, with 90 percent of them being between twelve and twenty years old.[3]

In his role as chairman of the Northern Uganda Task Force, Zac Niringiye was appointed to moderate an assembly of thirty local representatives in Lira, a city in northern Uganda and the fourth largest in the country. I was thrilled when Zac suggested that I accompany him on the six-hour drive from Kampala to Lira, because it would afford me precious one-on-one time with the mzee. I was eager to learn about the global church in Uganda and Africa, and I hoped to talk to him about my Global Church Listening Tour.

My wife would not have been supportive of my trip to the conflict region … if, that is, she had known about it. Myself, I was aware of some level of risk, but I was mostly eager for the extended visit with Zac.

As our van bounced and careened down the rutted dirt highway, I received a world-class graduate course in Mutuality. Zac explained Uganda's tribal history, the impact of colonialism, and how the nation continues to be crippled as a result. He emphasized the current vitality and power of Uganda's church, warning me that I must never equate economic or political weakness with spiritual frailty. He railed against the ways—visible and invisible, formal and informal, random and institutionalized—that Christians from powerful countries fail to esteem and treat Africans as equals. And then, when we finally arrived at Lira and the peace talks, I got to see him practice what he had preached.

"Electricity, hot water, food is ok, poor service" is what a generous Web site review said about our meeting site, which was also the hotel where we stayed. The White House Hotel, a cement compound with jumbles of exposed electrical wires and cinder block walls topped with broken glass shards, sat right on a busy dirt road in the middle of the bustling city block with colorful shops and crowded stalls on every side. Centrally located and well-known throughout the region, the White House was a perfect venue for the business at hand. At the center of the hotel was a courtyard with an outdoor stairway leading up to an open-air meeting room, which is where the talks were held. The room's levered window slats let in a welcome breeze—as well as the street sounds of car horns, music from humongous amplifiers, the shouts of merchants, and the squawks of chickens.

During the talks, the delegates frequently pulled their desk chairs into circles or huddled in corners of the room to work out one point or another. Much more like a deal closing than a touchy-feely dialogue, the talks surprised me in the measured, dispassionate focus on details. To me, it looked like "peace by logistics" as they haggled over myriad points that needed resolution before progress could occur:

- What routes could be protected and guaranteed to be safe for refugees in transit back to their newly peaceful villages?

- If the LRA soldiers were to evacuate from the northern region, where would they go, and would they be granted amnesty there?

- What forms of restitution would the LRA be willing to offer to victims?

- What forms of restitution would victims demand from the LRA?

- What timeline would the peace talks establish for the LRA's withdrawal from the northern region?

- Where would village-level peace talks be conducted, and when?

- What village representatives should be engaged to champion the peace process?

- If soldiers wished to leave the LRA and return to their home villages in northern Uganda, how should village leaders balance justice with reconciliation and reassimilation?

Just a glance around the meeting room signaled the difficulty of the task facing Rev. Niringiye. The assembled group included Muslims and Christians, national government officials and regional separatists, military officers, LRA victims, and LRA sympathizers. I saw a variety of army uniforms, Muslim robes and caps, African flowing shirts, natty European suits, Anglican cassocks, khakis, and jeans. While disorienting to me, this crazy array of characters, baggage, and agendas was right in Zac's sweet spot. And it called loud and clear for Mutuality.

During the two days of workmanlike attention to logistics, there were several tense points when the stakes heightened and voices rose. Just like with quietly feuding family members who harbor below-the-surface resentments and long-standing grudges, tensions threatened several times to erupt over one issue or another. Not surprisingly, Zac was thoroughly familiar with those acrimonious issues, and he explained them to me during breaks or on the ride home. These were complex matters, and not at all obvious to me as an outsider:

- Northern Ugandans are bitterly suspicious and resentful of the national government down south. Uganda is a country composed of many tribes, and the concerns of the Acholi tribe in northern Uganda figured especially prominently in these talks. This was no wonder, since over 90 percent of all Acholis were living in IDP camps in search of safety and security from the war at the time of the talks.[4]

- The International Criminal Court (ICC) in The Hague had already issued several indictments against Kony and his henchmen, an act which northern Ugandans viewed as meddling with their national sovereignty and self-determination. In addition to various subtle backstories,[5] Ugandans suspected that international politics were being allowed to determine the fate of millions of people living out unduly short lives in IDP camps.[6]

- The Acholi tribe does not subscribe to European or American principles of dispute resolution. I was taken aback, talking to several elected officials over dinner, to hear them side with Kony and not Kampala ... even though they *all* had lost close relatives to the LRA. As an American whose legal system is based on truth and justice,[7] I had no framework for understanding the centuries-old Acholi emphasis on forgiveness, reconciliation, and restoration. A matter that previously seemed to me so straightforward now looked impossibly complex. So I watched closely as Zac commiserated deeply with northern Ugandans who had seen their children commandeered into the LRA, later to be killed by the Ugandan army.[8]

- Most fundamentally, northern Ugandans feared that the indictments might trigger a fresh wave of revenge-based attacks by the LRA.

As a high official in Uganda's Anglican church, Zac did not shrink from exercising his clout and issuing pragmatic-yet-bold directives to all parties: "[W]e have got to be able to dialogue. Kony is a lunatic, a witch, all of these evil things. He depends on evil spirits. We must isolate him. Although one can't dialogue with someone who cannot accept reason, there has to be a way out of violence."[9]

I read an interview where Zac said that power is an enemy of Mutuality and often an enemy of Jesus Christ, and that Christians in power must view the world differently and read the Bible differently. Where there used to be a zero-sum game, Mutuality pursues a win-win result. Leaders must intentionally install processes that include new and varied voices, relying upon God to achieve His desired results through them as they pursue Mutuality. Like Jesus, we need to open ourselves to people without education, wealth, or contacts, and we must not seek power in order to ensure that ministry is done on our terms. Mutuality requires concessions and intentionality on the parts of all players, and this is especially difficult for the people with a voice and access to power.[10] Although it was in a Ugandan context that I saw these Mutuality lessons applied, I know that they are just as pertinent in cross-cultural contexts everywhere—whether on the international stage or in my increasingly diverse neighborhood in Richmond.

With his unique command both of African sympathies and international contingencies, Zac Niringiye was the perfect mediator to ground the Lira talks in Mutuality.[11] So, too, the global church is uniquely positioned in coming years as a champion of Mutuality. Sitting in Lira's White House Hotel, six hours away from the completely different world of Kampala, let alone Richmond, I recalled Zac's comments in an interview: "I have come to the conclusion that the powerful, those at the center, must begin to realize that the future shape of things does not belong to them. The future shape of things is on the periphery. The future shape of things is not in Jerusalem, but outside. It is Nazareth. It is Antioch. If you really want to understand the future of Christianity, go and see what is happening in Asia, Africa, Latin America.... God very often is working most powerfully far from the center."[12]

———————

Rev. Niringiye's point about the importance of learning from people in less-developed countries, far from the center of power, was the essence of the Listening Tour. Several months after meeting him, I got another powerful lesson in Mutuality in Cuzco, Peru.

Sitting on the steps of the Cathedral of Santo Domingo, I watched as the late afternoon sun cast long shadows on the bustling plaza in front of me. Situated at 11,000 feet in the Andes, Cuzco is a tourist magnet because of its colonial Spanish architecture and an abundance of trekking, rafting, and other outdoor activities. The town was settled in the eleventh century and sacked by Francisco Pizarro in 1533. As I admired the local residents ambling home from work across the cobblestoned square, I guessed that the scene looked much the same as it had several centuries ago.

One of the traps for an American abroad is to assume that a village or city has always relied on tourism for its meager economy, failing to recognize its rich history of accomplishment or how it has thrived in past times. For instance, I could see that Cuzco was quaint and charming, but I had not known that it was once a world center, counted among such cities as Athens, Vienna, Rome, Seville, Peking, and London.[13]

In the same way, it is easy to assume that people in poorer countries are lacking in expertise, intellect, or strategy—a bias that is the very opposite of Mutuality. Mutuality calls for recognizing the giftedness of others, deferring to them when appropriate, and providing leadership if helpful. An encounter with a remarkable Peruvian woman further convinced me of the need to practice Mutuality with indigenous leaders.

For three days in Cuzco, I observed thirty church leaders as they huddled in a bare cement storefront church, receiving training in planting rural churches. The teachers passed out photocopied handouts, and it seemed most of the students could read passably. They sat on cold benches, bundled in wool blankets and intently soaking in the lessons. Together they honed their preaching skills by delivering practice sermons and providing group feedback.

All of the gathered leaders were indigenous, and many had walked half a day or more from remote mountain villages outside Cuzco. They were all bivocational, with paying jobs in addition to their commitment to doing ministry work on the side, so they were not dependent on funds from Colorado Springs, London, Southern California, or Seoul. Meeting their own physical needs was not their concern; what they mostly yearned for was more biblical education and pastoral training. For several years, the Peruvians had benefitted from a Chicago-based group that trains Christian leaders in remote places, and that was what brought all of us to the cold, cement church in Cuzco.

I met Marcelina Huaman during one training session. Tiny and soft-spoken, she had the burnished skin common to people who live in high-altitude settings. Like the other women in the class, she had jet-black hair braided on each side and connected in the back to form a loop. When she walked outside, she added a wide-brimmed dark wool hat to her brightly patterned sweater, alpaca skirt, dark leggings, and plain walking shoes—typical dress for the high Andes.

Hardly typical in any other way, this woman stood out because of her intensity. It became clear that she was afforded special respect among her classmates. She spoke softly but with great authority, literally brimming with conviction, courage, and boldness. On my own, I could not comprehend her Spanish sermon, but I could tell that she was different from the others.

I wasn't wrong. As the first girl in her town to complete the third grade, Marcelina Huaman had shown leadership potential from a young age. In her teens she was influenced by the writings of Lenin, Marx, and Mao Zedong, and joined a political labor group for female domestic workers. She was recruited at age eighteen to join a cell group for The Shining Path, a Peru-based Maoist guerilla force that killed or kidnapped thirty-eight thousand Peruvians between 1970 and 1992.

In the factory where she worked, while she was enlisting new recruits to the communist cause, two women befriended Marcelina and gave her a Bible. After observing the two women and working alongside them, Marcelina eventually embraced their Christian faith at the age of twenty-four.

In her forty-six years, Marcelina had witnessed the widest range of philosophies and worldviews that Peru had to offer. Even since becoming a Christian and dedicating herself to ministry, she constantly encountered a Christianity diluted by centuries of confused theology and practice. Local Peruvian villagers mixed Catholicism with folk religion, ancient Incan rituals, occultism, and animism, sanctioning animal sacrifices, witch doctors, and worship of the sun or other gods. Generations of syncretism weakened the Peruvian church immeasurably, as people who claimed the name of Christ blended traits from all of the various religious perspectives and called it "Christianity."

Ministry in Peru requires grounded conviction and clear instruction—qualities with which Marcelina burns. It requires a commitment to mentoring—to showing cultural Christians how to reject counterfeit religious practices and pursue authentic relationships with Christ and other believers. Mentoring is a life-on-life process, not possible through books or apologetic teachings in oral-based Peru.

Who better to train beginning church planters for difficult missions than a former Maoist terrorist? Who better to cut through the numbness to real Christianity than someone who used to be the opponent? Who better to defy local superstitions and cultural traditions than someone accustomed to operating at great risk in the shadows of society? And, who better to be an ambassador for the power of the gospel than a former guerilla recruiter transformed by God's grace?

I have rarely seen such bold conviction as I saw in that five-foot woman. From my experience and exposure, the people who are most amply endowed with character and conviction are often ones who lack material wealth. As time and time again I meet people like Marcelina whose spiritual strength and character exceeds my own, I have developed immense respect for indigenous Christian leaders. The Peruvian body of Christ does not need America or other countries to lead it; rather, it needs its indigenous people to be equipped and mobilized for leadership. This reinforces what the Listening Tour respondents told us—the very best role for outside Christians is to train indigenous followers of Christ.

C. B. Samuel, Zac Niringiye, and Marcelina Huaman are powerful examples of moral and spiritual strength, the likes of which I have too rarely seen in Western Christian circles. God is indeed working very power-fully in such people, far from the center, and I need what they have ... and I find that to be indescribably encouraging.

Marcelina Huaman will probably never visit my office in Richmond, Virginia. She has probably never set foot in any suburb or office park, and that is even more reason that people like her should help to guide the global church into its next era.

If she were ever to come to Richmond, though, I am certain she would approve of my maps. Two maps hang on the wall of my confer-ence room. One is the traditional world map that we see in American classrooms. It shows the Western hemisphere at the left of the map, with North America at the top left. Not coincidentally, that is where readers from countries in the West first look when they read a page. That makes North America easy and fast to find, the natural starting point of the map.

The world map does not have to be arranged that way. If the mapmaker had simply flipped all the countries around, then west would be on the right of the map and north would be at the bottom. In that layout, Australia would be at the top and center of the map...which is precisely how my second map looks. Called an "Upside-Down Map," it is produced—not surprisingly—in Sydney, Australia. Tired of the traditional Western layout, the Aussies righted (or uprighted) that bias.

The point of the upside-down map is to give the position of honor to "global south" countries. Not a term in wide circulation, "global south" was coined in academic circles but is coming into extensive usage among global affairs and missions experts. It generally includes impoverished countries that are mostly in the southern hemisphere and not in North America or Europe. Those countries used to be designated as "third world countries," and sometimes still are designated as "developing countries" or "underdeveloped countries." Today, they may be called "two-thirds world countries" or "the majority world" (because a majority of the world is underdeveloped).[14] Whatever the designation for the region, one thing is clear about it: Christianity is thriving there.

It is also very important to clarify what is meant by the "West" or "Western countries." When international relations discussions, including those about missions, refer to the West, the reference is usually intended to denote the countries of Western Europe, the United States, and Canada.[15]

A shift of the nucleus of Christendom from the West to the global south has been widely documented and discussed in mission circles. In Africa, professing Christians numbered just 10 million in 1900, but had remarkably spread to 360 million by 2000. While Africa was home to just 1.6 percent of the world's Christians in 1500, today 18 percent live there, and by 2025 that figure should be just under 25 percent. The same trends are sweeping through Latin America and Asia.[16]

The Christianity practiced in the global south is often different from that Western churches. Many Christians in the global south view American and European controversies over ordination of gay pastors and gay marriage as ludicrous. Their literal reading of the Bible leads them to regard those practices as utter heresy. Taking the Bible literally, they believe in the power of prayer, in healing and other spiritual gifts, and in the good that comes from suffering. Believers in the global south also often display explicit passion and fervor in their worship.[17]

Global mission efforts in the past may have been aimed at "the uncivilized," but that model will not prove relevant in the future. In countries like India and China, where rural dwellers are flocking to cities and the middle class is rapidly growing, the unreached are just as likely to live in urban slums as rural villages. Indeed, Indian mission experts today are deeply concerned about the dearth of young Indian missionaries able to reach out to middle- or upper-class Indians.[18]

As a result of the increasingly empowered global south, what used to be called the "mission field"—those people whom Christian missionaries went out to reach with the gospel of Jesus—now sends out missionaries of its own. The mission field today has become entirely multidirectional. At a 1987 conference of Ibero-American mission leaders in São Paolo, evangelist Luis Bush boldly declared Latin America to be a mission force and no longer a mission field. The 7 Currents usually interrelate with and support each other, and this is a case in point. Mutuality is forced and fostered by multidirectional missions today, which is made possible by the Global Current of Migration.

British scholar Chris Wright addresses the multidirectional nature of the mission movement: "[Y]ou are as likely to meet a Brazilian missionary in North Africa as a British missionary in Brazil.... Mission today is from everywhere, to everywhere."[19] Formerly, American Christians often felt that foreign missions necessarily involved crossing an ocean, but that "saltwater missiology" is obsolete today. Today, American Christians need to readjust their thinking of missions as something we go to "over there," in light of the fact that the "ends of the earth" have come over here.[20]

An Asian pastor friend of mine comes to the United States every few years. Over the course of a few weeks, he connects with friends who support his ministry through money, prayer, and friendship. He enjoys sharing with Americans the ways that God uses their support to help him mentor his country's Christian leaders, particularly university students. A few years ago, he planned to visit the American church that was his largest annual financial supporter.

This kind of trip to the United States is common. In the broad context of philanthropy around the world, Americans are uniquely generous with their financial resources; religiously motivated donors give the most of all.[21] That generosity extends far, as faith-driven American donors support not only their local churches but also Christian work around the world.

Relationships between Western donors and ministries in the global south are complicated, though. Mutuality proves especially challenging when money is involved. All too often, relationships mimic common wisdom and secular patterns rather than biblical standards. Unfortunately, the Golden Rule that is practiced is not the biblical "do unto others as you would have them do unto you," but the secular "he who has the gold makes the rules." Donors can come to feel like owners, and Christian workers like hired hands, for "he who pays the piper calls the tune." The result can be arrogance and mistrust among donors, and resentment and suspicion among receivers.

My Asian friend recounted to me, "I called on the church to meet with the pastors to thank them for their gift, as I had done on previous visits. I had hoped to fill them in on new developments in my ministry of preaching at churches, training staffs, coaching leaders, and much more. I had hoped to pray with them and for them; to share challenges and wisdom and, perhaps, a cup of tea.

"The church had several pastors on staff, but none were able to meet with me. The entire staff was on a retreat, and the schedules just did not work out. Neither was it possible, apparently, to meet with members of the church's mission committee."

He shared with me his displeasure, for that situation did not feel at all like Mutuality to him. He had never viewed provision of funds by a church as a one-way transaction, but more like a relationship where each party was able to give to the other. He had never intended to take someone's money without also sharing their lives—their hopes, needs, questions, and insights. He was not interested in charity, but rather in an exchange.

"I want to give that money back," he continued, "if it will not be accompanied by a relationship." I asked him how much money was involved, and it turned out that the church's support amounted to more than 60 percent of his annual budget. That did not matter one bit to him. "I can get that money elsewhere," he laughingly told me. That made me feel small, because I knew he was right. Once again, I was being schooled by a global south Christian leader, this time on a classic American weakness—faith in money instead of God. "The money is not the church's, it is God's," he continued. "If God wants me to have that money for His work, He will give it to me through one source or another."

His reaction turned my preconceptions upside down. From the perspective of Mutuality, though, it made great sense. He was a man of experience, accomplishment, and deep spiritual strength, humbly asking Westerners for money. Like every ministry worker from the global south, he was keenly aware of the inequities of wealth, access, and power. He wanted to be in a relationship with his American donors, and he knew that God desired for the money flow to bring Christians from different worlds into relationships with each other. Once in relationship, my friend looked forward to listening, teaching, serving, and leading in ways he was trained to do as a pastor. He could give, then, from his spiritual wealth, in order to meet the needs of those who were giving from their financial wealth.

He perceived, though, that his American friends did not understand that their relationship could and should extend beyond simply giving money to poor foreign Christian workers. He felt that the American church overvalued the abundant capital that it controlled, and undervalued the by-product that he cared about most—the relationship, without which he saw no value in the money transfer.

The pastor was clearly frustrated, and I was surprised by his intensity. "I might just cut that church off from supporting me," he warned. That was a new one to me—a ministry leader talking about cutting off a donor! I had not even considered how that was possible. In my experience, it had always been the prerogative of the party with money to cut off the party without money, but never vice versa.

Clearly, though, some things get turned upside down in a world of Mutuality. In that world, poor Asian pastors cut off wealthy American churches. Imagine that.

In the global church's future, Christian leaders from the global south will demand dignity and Mutuality. They will demand Mutuality for ministry leaders, societal outcasts, victims of disasters, or countrymen of other religions, for they know that God is not a respecter of position. They will be less and less intimidated by money, titles, technology, mobility, and institutions, and they will display more and more of the spiritual authority invested in them by God.

I have learned my most profound lessons about Mutuality from my friends in the global south. Western Christians are no longer in control of the global church, but now stand among many important and gifted players.

As an American, I am humbly proud of the leadership my countrymen have provided to the global church in years past and also the very important role we will play in the future. During the Global Church Listening Tour, respondents repeatedly expressed enthusiastic appreciation for Americans' optimism, encouragement, generosity of spirit, and honesty. They also recognized the global church's ongoing reliance upon Westerners' administrative, project management, and training skills.

At the same time, Zac Niringiye pointed out to me that Westerners' perceived place in the center of God's plan—remember the traditional map we use?—has led us to believe that we are in charge. The future of Mutuality requires me to look at the world differently and to read the Bible differently. I must view other countries' Christian leaders as equals. I cannot view the West, or any country, as the beginning and center of the global church. The map has been turned upside down.

MUTUALITY
Representative Organizations

Organizations that seek to practice Mutuality must do more than merely establish token partnerships or hire token employees. Below are four ministries that are "hardwired" for Mutuality and have taken the hard steps all along the way. By no means are these groups immune to lapses into Western myopia, but they have altered their processes, timelines, budgets, and priorities to include new and divergent voices.

1. **John Stott Ministries:** Since 1969, John Stott Ministries (JSM) has helped to finance the education of promising developing-world scholars at prominent Western universities and seminaries. JSM's founder, Dr. John Stott, has been one of the intellectual driving forces of the evangelical global church for decades. His writing, his preaching, and JSM all combine to educate, equip, and empower Christian scholars from the global south for service in their home countries. (www.JohnStott.org)

2. **International Fellowship of Mission Theologians:** In the early 1990s, Dr. Vinay Samuel founded the International Fellowship of Mission Theologians (INFEMIT). An Indian pastor and early JSM scholarship recipient, Dr. Samuel had long lamented the lack of global south participation—let alone leadership—in scholarly matters. He built networks of promising young scholars in Africa, Asia, and Latin America, all who lacked resources and mentors. Since its founding, INFEMIT has blossomed into a community of scholars from throughout the global south, embodying the rich potential that lies in store for a global church defined by Mutuality. (www.ocms.ac.uk)

83

3. **International Mission Board:** In 1997, the International Mission Board (IMB) announced to the global church that it was committed to a new, more collaborative model of ministry. As the world's largest mission agency, IMB had a 152-year history of leadership in the global church ... and also a reputation around the world for "going it alone." IMB's president, Dr. Jerry Rankin, acknowledged the problem and championed a "new spirit of global cooperation and synergy."[22] Today, IMB is increasingly recognized as an eager partner with indigenous organizations and other mission agencies. (www.imb.org)

4. **Word Made Flesh:** Since 1991, Word Made Flesh (WMF) has sent followers of Christ around the world to live with "friends"— the poorest of the poor in Argentina, Bolivia, Brazil, India, Moldova, Nepal, Peru, Romania, Sierra Leone, and Thailand. By seeking to understand root causes of poverty and identifying with those living with prostitution, disease, addiction, and more, WMF works for transformation in impoverished communities. (www.wordmadeflesh.org)

CHAPTER 4

Migration

A Taste of Heaven

The world changed on September 11. With the murder of three thousand people, that day instantly became a hideous benchmark for terror and religious extremism. The architect of the attack called it "the righteous judgment of God on these barbarous wretches, who have imbued their hands with so much innocent blood." He prayed that God would have all the glory.

The date was September 11, 1649, and Oliver Cromwell was the commander of the British army's massacre of Drogheda, Ireland.[1] The British Parliament had ordered Cromwell and his Protestant troops to subdue Catholic Ireland, and Drogheda was one of the first cities he faced. The death toll included seven hundred civilians and priests, some burned inside of St. Peter's Church where they had taken refuge.

I first visited Drogheda in 1978. A blue-collar city just thirty miles north of Dublin, it was a microcosm of a country where very little had gone well since Cromwell. Drogheda, like Ireland, had been sacked and looted. Its economy relied all too heavily on agriculture, often subsistence farming. Its people had suffered through intermittent famines and constant poverty. Hordes of citizens had emigrated elsewhere, but few outsiders had ever come *to* Ireland. Those who did, like Cromwell, came for the purpose of marauding, dominating, and extracting.

When I returned to the city in 2006, though, I saw a completely different Ireland.

It seems that, after a few millennia at the short end of every stick, the Emerald Isle finally met prosperity. In addition to the fertile farmlands, beautiful green and tan quilt-like fields, and ancient stone walls, there were now ubiquitous outcroppings of McMansions that owed more to Dallas than to Dublin.

A journalist wrote that Ireland had "catapulted itself in a few decades from beer-soaked backwater to the Celtic Tiger whose growth rates, foreign investment and rags-to-riches story were the envy of every languishing small nation with a thirst for a makeover."[2] The "Celtic Tiger" was the nickname given to the country's wildly resurgent economy, which surged in the 1990s, slowed in 2001, and took off again from 2003 until 2007. The boom experienced during that period transformed Ireland from one of Europe's poorer countries into one of its wealthiest.[3]

People from all around the world took notice and set their stake in Ireland.[4] Multinational corporations like Dell, Intel, Hewlett-Packard, and Amazon moved there, lured by relatively low wages, government grants, low tax rates, farm subsidies, access for foreign investors to the European Union (EU) market, and the young, educated, English-speaking labor force. Microsoft, Google, Yahoo, and PayPal set up their European headquarters in Dublin.

The Ireland of the past—agrarian, downtrodden, and ethnically homogeneous—was giving way. One Drogheda resident told me that new immigrants were visible all throughout the city's day-to-day life, with different nationalities gravitating toward different jobs: the butchers were Brazilian, the petrol-station attendants were Chinese, and the farm workers were Russian. All of those new arrivals in Ireland are key players in the third Global Current—*Migration.*

Ireland's medieval roots have always fascinated me, and during my most recent visit to Drogheda I was eager to return to Monasterboice. It is a place that symbolizes for me what was once a country known for its piety. A monastic settlement dating back to the sixth century, Monasterboice is world-renowned among art historians for its massive stone high crosses. Locals are so used to the ancient graveyard and ruins, though, that there is little more than a garden gate and some nondescript educational markers to denote its presence. (Until recently, the skeleton key to the sixty-foot round tower could be found in a side shed.) The showpiece of Monasterboice is the remarkably preserved fifteen-foot Muiredach's Cross, with a shaft, cross arm, and ring carved full of Celtic interlace and spirals, geometric patterns, vinery, and biblical depictions. Irish high crosses, like stained-glass windows several centuries later, were tools that the learned priesthood used to teach Bible stories to their illiterate flock.

As I marveled at the extraordinary religious artwork, I mused about how central Christianity was to Irish life for so long … and how far it had slid. One and a half millennia ago, Ireland's ancient Celtic church and its missionaries took the gospel to many nations in Europe. Irish people have endured centuries of oppression, violence, and bloodshed at the hands of the Vikings and the British, much of it because of religion. During the 1990s, the Catholic Church was weakened by high-profile scandals in the priesthood. Today, Irish people who once jammed cathedrals are staying home. Ireland appears to be one more European country where churches are being boarded up and turned into lofts, coffeehouses, or museums.[5]

That is why I never imagined looking to Ireland for insights into today's global church. Not until I attended a conference on men's ministry in Orlando, Florida, where I caught wind of one of the most innovative and original churches I had ever encountered.

Along with about seventy-five Americans at the conference, there was a delegation of four Irishmen. I was quite intrigued that a place called the Solid Rock Multicultural Pentecostal Church, located in the heart of post-Christian Ireland, would send four laymen to a training conference in America. My curiosity was further piqued when I saw that two of the four men were African immigrants. That did not seem like the Ireland I remembered.

After returning from that Orlando conference, I found myself thinking of Ireland often … and in a new light. I was surprised to come across an article by a Tennessee seminary professor referring to the very same Solid Rock Church.

Then Easter Sunday sealed the deal. Every year, my hometown of Richmond closes off its main boulevard for a ten-block Easter parade—really much more of an extended block party. It is always a festive event, with bands, street performers, and contests for the best bonnets and pet costumes. Amid blooming azaleas and dogwoods, and people in their Sunday best or their just-unpacked shorts and sandals, I saw a couple in African garb looking decidedly lost. When my children saw their dad heading in the direction of an international couple, they cringed. It would be a while, they knew, because I love meeting people from other countries and hearing their stories.

While driving through Richmond on their way south, the man and his wife had been rerouted because of the parade. I pointed them in the right direction and, of course, struck up a conversation. I learned that Obert Dumi and Patience Tafuma were originally from Zimbabwe, had immigrated to Ireland, and had joined a church there that had many African immigrants. I shouldn't have been surprised to learn that their church was Solid Rock Church!

Solid Rock has many programs in place to welcome and assimilate immigrants like Obert and Patience into the church community. According to respondents to the Global Church Listening Tour, massive Migration today presents the opportunity to welcome immigrants into worshipping communities throughout the United States and the world. A related observation was that refugees and immigrants from the global south are bringing fresh fervor and devoutness to Western countries. All of that is just what was happening in Ireland.

Friends of mine who are birders will travel great distances to see rare or exotic species. I was now completely intrigued by multiple sightings of an exotic early twenty-first-century Christian species—a Christian church thriving in post-Christian Western Europe. My interest sufficiently piqued, I resolved to make email contact with its pastor, Nick Park. One thing led to another, until I ended up in Drogheda on a miserable, wet June weekend.

In the cold drizzle, I tried to follow the cryptic directions Pastor Nick had given me to Solid Rock Church. Driving on winding country lanes lined by hedgerows, and then through the tired, blue-collar city, I passed Drogheda Rugby Club and took a wrong turn into Callahan's scrap metal yard. Right after that, I located the church's drab metal building in a muddy, fenced-in cluster of warehouses. It was no cathedral.

There were about four hundred people worshipping that Sunday, at least half of whom were immigrants, mostly from Africa. Out of six hundred members of that church, a minority were Irish nationals. The immigrant members came from thirty-four nations, predominantly Nigeria, Ghana, Zimbabwe, and India. It was a working-class congregation, and a few men I talked to proudly told me that the congregants had done the wiring and carpentry work to convert the warehouse into a worship area.

At the same time, I noted that the different nationalities affirmed and interacted with each other freely and warmly. They appeared to be true partners in Solid Rock Church—whether gathering in worship, going out in ministry, or partying (Africans and Irish both do that well!) in fellowship.

Afterward, I waited as Pastor Nick and his wife Janice mingled with the congregation. As a stiff, white American visitor, I felt conspicuously "other" amid the pan-African after-church hubbub. Obert and Patience spotted me immediately and, returning my hospitality from the previous Easter, rushed over to hug me.

Nick, knowing that we would never get a chance to talk uninterrupted at the church, kindly suggested that we steal away to a village pub. "Is there any problem with going into a pub … you know, as a pastor?" I asked him. "Oh no," he said, "not at all. I've spent a lot of time in pubs … too much, in fact. I won't be having any beer, mind you, but it will give us a place to chat."

No cloistered man of the cloth, Nick is a recovering alcoholic. With Irish people—a "show me" bunch who know blarney when they hear it—I guessed that Nick's flawed background provides credibility.

I learned a great deal about the state of Ireland and the Irish church, though only a portion of our conversation dealt with religion, faith, or spirituality. That is not because Nick Park is shy about his faith. Nor is he a postmodern European who has intellectualized all of the power and wonder out of Christianity. To the contrary, he is a Pentecostal pastor who believes deeply that God, His Son, and the Holy Spirit are moving powerfully in Drogheda and the world today. He shares good news with the urgency of a saved man tossing a lifeline to drowning people.

He explained to me, "My sermons are always Bible-centered. Skeptics— and Ireland is full of them—are put off by patronizing 'Christianity lite' approaches, but they're attracted by doctrinal clarity. I'm absolutely convinced about the power of preaching God's Word in the face of any opposition or circumstances. After all, that's why my wife and I chose Drogheda for our first church—because it had the highest unemployment and teen suicide rates in the country."

Nick Park has planted thirteen churches in Ireland in as many years. Why and how, I wondered, were his church planting efforts so fruitful in a country of such spiritual barrenness?

"From my first days as a pastor," he began, "I felt called to do ministry differently."

Nick and I saw eye to eye. "It seems that, if you had stuck with the timeworn Irish approaches to religion," I suggested, "your church would be as empty as Dublin's grand cathedrals are today." It seemed to me that Irish people today aren't buying what the traditional church is selling.

What impressed me most was how he understood Ireland's culture as it was being changed by dramatic influences both from within and without its borders. He was both instinctive and intentional in identifying cultural trends. Not for a second did he assume that today's culture was the same as when he grew up in Northern Ireland, or the same as the one in which his daughter would live. He constantly considered a wide array of global areas in flux—sociology, religious history, demographics, philosophy, marketing, economics, missiology, and more—in order to gain a current understanding of complex issues. He browsed atheist Web sites regularly to learn how to communicate with youth on the streets of Drogheda. And, every day, he studied the Bible.

Nick was practicing information arbitrage—looking at the world from many perspectives. Nick Park has much to teach the global church, for information arbitrage will be as essential in the future in remote Latin American jungles, teeming Asian cities, and African slums as it is today in bustling developed-world settings like Dublin.

Back in the pub, Nick blurted out, "I categorically believe that every aspect of my ministry is influenced by Migration in Ireland. Mainstream business writers in London, Tokyo, and New York all have focused on the Celtic Tiger, but I believe that ministry in Ireland is all about Migration." He underscored his point with the bold claim, "Migration is *the* key moral issue of our day. It used to be slavery, then integration, then abortion. Now it is immigration."[6] That was a new idea to me, so I listened even more carefully; I was getting better at listening, the more I tried it.

Nick had a deep, heart-level interest in immigration. "In 1994, when we started Solid Rock, Drogheda's diversity was near zero percent. The only black people then were nuns or missionaries. Now, between ten and fifteen percent of the people in Ireland are immigrants." Ireland's population has grown rapidly, too, to its highest level in a long time—since 1861, to be exact![7] For Nick Park and Solid Rock Church, population growth and immigration are nothing if not opportunities to share and to love.

Nick explained his strategies for reaching out to nearby immigrants:

> At Solid Rock, we are very intentional about reaching out to the immigrants flooding Drogheda, to learn the cultural assumptions and expectations that they bring with them. We then use those customs as bridges, establishing a rapport across language and cultural differences. Unlike Irish nationals, the immigrants are generally open to church and faith.
>
> With Nigerian parishioners, I attend their baby-naming parties and bless them on their eighth day. Those parties are a counterpart to the Muslim tradition of circumcising baby boys on their eighth day.
>
> When I read in the newspaper that Ireland was actively recruiting Filippino nurses, I thought about how we might minister to them. We decided to contact a sister church in the Philippines and convinced them to send a missionary to Dublin for those OFWs (Overseas Filipino Workers).
>
> Within a few kilometers of Solid Rock stands a former summer camp, now used as a camp for refugees from the Balkan conflict. Naturally, our parishioners wondered how we might reach out to them. We found ways to help in meeting the

many physical and spiritual needs of immigrants
in that camp. On one Sunday, I dedicated twenty-
seven infant children of camp residents.

"Very little inside or outside of your church seems to remain static," I
noted. "That's right," Nick responded. "You see, the Christian church too
often reacts to change, when it should be anticipating it. We try to make
that kind of entrepreneurial, opportunistic outreach a part of the culture
at Solid Rock."

Nick and his church have even turned age-old missionary funding
models on their head. It is typical for ministries around the world to send
representatives to the United States to raise money, but that approach is
not without its problems. Insiders in the ministry world and also in aid
communities recognize that many donations from abroad are Band-Aid
gifts that create dependency on outside support. Especially for countries
which have been under colonial rule, that money stream can perpetuate
more problems than it solves.

"Solid Rock," Nick told me, "puts a fresh twist on that pattern. A
member of Solid Rock's staff travels to the U.S. every year to visit relatives. He takes several trunks with him, fills them with bargain clothes
that he buys at T. J. Maxx or another discount store, sells the clothes
back in Ireland, and uses the profit to cover his personal support as a
missionary." In that way, Nick explained, that person generates his own
support without having to solicit funds from the poor immigrants he's
serving. Nick seeks opportunities to exhort his flock to generous giving,
but not in this case.

What powerful symbolism that the steamer trunk—long used by
Western missionaries to take all of their possessions to live in foreign
lands—is now a tool for generating profit and self-support! This is typical of the empowering, resourceful, enterprising approach that Nick Park
brings to ministry.

If a person in a cauldron of change like Drogheda claimed never to be uncertain or discouraged, I would be suspicious. Nick Park admits to his share of misgivings and missteps. In the Sunday service I attended, he taught, "Too many Christians are afraid to fail. It is important to take risks, and it is okay to fail. I want Solid Rock to be a place where people feel free to fail." But his innovations have been right much more often than not. Solid Rock's congregations in the Republic of Ireland total 3500 members. Two of the congregations are French-speaking Congolese, four are Romanian (two specifically for ethnic gypsies), two Russian, three Brazilian, and … oh yes, there are two English-speaking congregations. One of the Romanian gatherings, with nine hundred members, is the largest Protestant congregation in the Republic of Ireland.

Nick is gratified by the fruit as he fulfills the mission given to him: "My greatest joy," he said, "is seeing all of the different nationalities together. It is a taste of heaven."

———————

Migration is the human face of globalization. Physical and spiritual crises proliferate in the globalizing world, and increasing numbers of people are fleeing their home countries in search of better lives. Some leave because of "push" factors (famine, natural catastrophes, war, oppression, and poverty in their home country) and others because of "pull" factors (food, peace, liberty, and prosperity elsewhere).[8] They are part of a massive Global Current, yet each immigrant has distinct personal histories, hopes, and needs. Immigrants are also uniquely open to outreach. Now is the time for the global church to find new ways to be a winsome and life-giving witness to immigrants of God's love for them.[9]

Working together as they often do, the Currents are potent forces. The Global Current of Machines, with global transportation increasingly afford able to the masses, is contributing to extraordinary levels of Migration. The Global Current of Monoculture, with newspapers, magazines, television, and movies idealizing wealthy Western lifestyles, spurs the world's poor to seek their own good life, often away from home.[10]

For dirt-poor North Africans looking northward, southern Spain is the prized portal to freedom and economic opportunity.[11] European Union officials call that coast Europe's "southern front line," and each year tens of thousands of illegal African immigrants set their sights on that shore.[12] The ones who fail lose their lives to the seas.

Those who succeed usually arrive in their new country with profound needs—both financial and psychological. They often bring with them scars from poverty, oppression, and conflict back home … and also memories of dangerous and traumatic immigration journeys. Those immigrants and their scars, again, are the human face of globalization.

With Spain's southern shores as their destination, they travel in canoes and "pateras" (low-floating boats) from North Africa to an embarkation point on the Canary Islands, off the coast of Morocco. In the process, there occurs a sort of "immigration gridlock," with large backlogs of people at several different locations. At one point in the summer of 2006, it was estimated that more than one hundred thousand immigrants were waiting for their chance to take the Senegal-to-Canaries leg of the journey. Among the various perils they confront, the weather and water conditions between North Africa and Gibraltar loom largest. Another obstacle is Spanish authorities, who use an electronic surveillance system and mobile units and routinely pick up several hundred floating undocumented immigrants daily during warm weather months. Migration is always traumatic and often perilous, and in this case death is a real risk: As many as 1,700 North Africans lose their lives every year in their quest for opportunity and freedom in Spain.[13]

Migration to and from Spain is nothing new. A week in the beautiful, historic city of Granada, Spain reminded me that Spain has long been a global hub, targeted from all directions.

I was in Granada to attend a weeklong conference on a fascinating growing trend in the global church: Christian workers from "new sending countries" in Latin America moving east to Africa, Europe, and Asia to assist struggling churches.[14] I was one of about two thousand global church leaders and missionaries at the conference, who traveled to Granada from thirty-seven countries, mostly in Latin America.

One evening I walked from my hotel toward the edge of town and the Alhambra, the incomparable Muslim fortress nestled in the majestic Sierra Nevada mountain range. Wandering through Granada's city center past the cathedral, I was reminded of Spain's status as a medieval superpower. She was admired, imitated, and feared worldwide for her technological innovation, economic strength, commercial prowess, and aggressive imperialism.

A grand statue commemorating Christopher Columbus's momentous audience with Queen Isabella in Granada drove home that point. Kneeling before the queen, the navigator lays out his maps and seeks her support for his journeys.[15] After shopping his exploration proposal around the courts of Europe for the better part of a decade, the evangel-explorer finally found a likeminded patron in the spiritually zealous queen.[16] Among a complex bundle of agendas, it is clear that Columbus and the queen had in common a goal of taking the gospel from Spain to all of the world.[17]

I realized, as I stared up at the massive monument, that the missionary vision of Isabella and Columbus had come full circle. More than five hundred years later and just a few blocks from that royal audience, thousands of people were gathered to explore ways to take the gospel from Columbus's former New World back to now-secular Western Europe and other places currently without vibrant church communities.

Like Columbus's and Isabella's plan, this new global church strategy reflected a vision of daring global scope. Both visions recognized the strategic importance of Spain, first as a westernmost launch point for the New World and now as a southern front line for Europe. And both initiatives—the Columbus-Isabella partnership and the global church's new "back at you" strategy—were premised on mobility and Migration.

Migration has always existed, but it has now increased in magnitude and complexity. It is occurring in all corners of the globe, and indigenous church communities must learn how to adapt to strangers in their midst. Migration poses a rash of challenges, most of which apply to Spanish Christian churches dealing with North African immigrants, Nick Park and Solid Rock Church, and American churches—if not this year, then some year soon:

1. Do national (indigenous) churches and ministries want to include or mix with immigrants? For instance, will immigrants be welcomed into Spanish churches?[18] Will it make a difference if the immigrants speak our language our way, or will there be prejudice or snobbery toward poorer "cousins"?[19] Will Irish churches welcome immigrants from India who also speak English?

2. How should national churches and ministries adapt and adjust (contextualize) their methods and messages to reach immigrants from other cultures? Even if immigrants do speak our language, should our stories, examples, and approaches be tailored for different cultural backgrounds? For ministries that produce evangelistic literature, should different materials be used, even if the language is the same?

3. Will national churches or ministries seek to mix national Christians and immigrants, or will each nationality have distinct worship services and organizations? In Drogheda, for instance, Solid Rock Church holds both distinct services for people from different countries and blended services.

4. Will national ministry leaders be willing to share leadership authority with immigrants, or will immigrants always be "on the receiving end" of ministry—regardless of spiritual maturity or education level?

5. Will national ministries seek to meet the inevitable physical needs of immigrants—food, shelter, clothing, education, literacy, language skills, and jobs? Or will national ministries solely concentrate on the spiritual lives of the immigrants? What societal stresses should national Christians anticipate and address in the immigrant communities?

6. Knowing that many immigrants (particularly from Latin America) choose to worship in evangelical and Pentecostal churches in their adopted country, and not the Catholic churches in which they were raised, will that cause additional tensions between Catholic and Protestant churches of all types?

Some of these issues have been around since biblical times, for the global church has always sought to contextualize its message for different cultures. Many issues, though, have distinctly modern twists in our global world, where Migration is forced on cultures at a pace and intensity previously unimaginable. Behind all of these issues is an unsettling but undeniable reality confronting the global church: Migration is no longer limited to the intrepid few globetrotters who are called or sent, but it is coming soon to a church near you.

———

As people migrate throughout the globe in search of better lives, they often head toward cities. They see cities as places that offer education, housing, jobs, entertainment, health care, and social services—and also anonymity and concentrations of fellow countrymen. Urbanization is one of the most profound expressions of Migration in the world today. Researchers' projections paint a dramatic picture of global urbanization. The twentieth century was the century of urbanization. In 1900, only 14 percent of the world lived in or near cities; today over half of us do.[20]

Over the course of the next two decades, the global urban population will double, from 2.5 to 5 billion, with almost all of that increase occurring in developing, non-Christian countries.[21] Tracked and analyzed by secular and Christian "urbanologists" for decades, urbanization is clearly a defining issue for today's global church.

Here lies a most unfortunate irony, though, where the global church is out of step. On one hand, the poor and disenfranchised of the world see cities as beacons of hope and a better life, and they leave families and security to migrate there. On the other, there is a strong history of Christian disdain toward cities as hotbeds of iniquity, travail, and turmoil.[22] Urbanization reads like a tale of two cities, and the global church finds itself once again at the Meeting of the Waters. In the process, Christians too often overlook one of the modern world's most bountiful and strategic ministry opportunities—urbanization.[23]

A hopeful, redemptive, and faithful view of cities sees vibrant places of opportunity, diversity, innovation, and new expressions of Christianity. Urban advocates point out that God has a high view of cities: In the Bible, man's journey begins in a perfect garden, but it ends in a recreated, holy city.[24]

The Reverend Tim Keller is the staunchest of city champions. In 1989, he moved with his family from small-town Virginia to then-bankrupt and violence-ridden New York City. Manhattan lacked a prominent, visible Christian community at the time, but Keller believed that cities were *the* strategic—and scriptural—mandate for the global church's future.

His vision and timing were right, and he has played an important role in the revitalization of the community of Christian churches in New York

City. He has been an agent for progress that was previously unthinkable: the emergence of a megachurch and a network of a hundred church plants in Manhattan, where his Redeemer Presbyterian Church now averages more than five thousand weekly worshippers at five sites. In addition, Keller has become one of the most influential voices in the evangelical American church, and his 2008 book, *The Reason for God,* rose as high as number seven on the *New York Times* nonfiction best-seller list.

A few years ago, Dr. Keller explained to me why the global church must turn its future focus on the world's cities. He noted that, in the past, international evangelization efforts focused on "unreached people groups."[25] He explained to me how Manhattan and other world-class cities are the new unreached people groups. As such, he argued, the world's major cities should be high priorities for the global church in its praying, working, sending, and giving.

Picturing New York City—or, for that matter, any of the world's major cities—as a needy unreached people group was a stretch for me. There at the Meeting of the Waters, I had to decide whether to adhere to traditional missions wisdom or to heed the 7 Global Currents and entertain new perspectives, for God's sake. When I previously thought of unreached people groups, I thought of tribes like the Waodani in Ecuador. The Waodani had never encountered white people, let alone Christianity, before five young missionary pilots dropped into their lives in 1956. The missionaries, who knew full well the tribe's violent reputation, were ambushed by spear- and machete-wielding Waodani.[26] The massacre, featured in a ten-page photo spread in *LIFE* magazine, was later redeemed when the martyrs' widows returned to live among the Waodani tribe. Those and other tales like it have motivated generations of Christians to take the gospel to all the world, which has traditionally been understood to mean unreached people groups comprised of unsophisticated and backward people living "in the bush."

"The future missionary call," Keller insisted, "should be *both* to the bush and to [New York City's] Flatbush." He explained to me that, in

Manhattan, we see all the classic elements of an unreached people group. First and foremost, a huge percentage of the citizenry has never been presented with the claims of Jesus Christ. Like all unreached people groups, Manhattan has its own philosophies and worldview—witness *Seinfeld, The Sopranos, Sex and the City,* Woody Allen movies, and so many other depictions that initially leave what they call "flyover America" (those unfortunate states that are neither New York nor California) mystified. New York has a unique language, and Keller acknowledges in his book that he intentionally communicates in a manner that resonates with naturally cynical and ironic New Yorkers.[27] Unreached people groups have unique customs, cultures, clothing, and food—and so does New York City. Finally, Keller said, New York is an unreached people group because there has historically been a grave lack of indigenous financial resources devoted to Christian ministry there, which leaves the Christian community dependent on outside financial investment and support.

"What," he challenged me, "could be more strategic and important than sewing revival in a world-class city like New York, which in turn shapes so much of the nation's and the world's culture?" He has long used his voice and influence to challenge Christians to become familiar and fluent in the issues and opportunities in today's cities. This particularly presents a challenge to the American church, where the white evangelical Protestants who control missions are overwhelmingly non-urban in background. They are skeptical about whether ministry in cities is worth the great cost, they don't appreciate the strategic nature of city ministry, and according to Keller they just don't like cities.

Cities can certainly present a scary image. Drugs, prostitution, and crime may appear to be easy alternatives for city dwellers with no other prospects. Housing demand exceeds supply, and overcrowding is the norm. And because of anonymity and mobility, cities often offer a weak social fabric. In China, millions of migrants flock to cities, only to encounter impersonal, coldly anonymous environments. Gone are the tight family-based rural communities; contacts and interactions are more often based on jobs, hobbies, or physical proximity.

The world's largest cities—especially those in the global south—are literally choked with air pollution. Garbage accumulates in slums, green spaces give way to cement, and noise and activity rarely cease. However, despite the deplorable conditions, the allure of cities persists and the migration will continue.[28] Vast slums and squatter camps are mushrooming throughout Latin America, Africa, and many parts of Asia. Some 924 million people, or 31.6 percent of the world's total urban population, live in urban slums.[29] By 2030, urban poverty is expected to impact up to half of all urban residents.[30]

How, then, should the global church respond?

An obvious first step will be for churches and Christians to stop fleeing. When Christians migrate to the suburbs, they leave urban areas with very little daily Christian presence and witness. The global church must recognize that Christians are the best hope to serve the inhabitants of modern global cities. In turn, modern cities present rich opportunities for inquiring and educated residents: a constant stream of ideas, debate, and education; art and architecture; government; potential for societal change; wealth and other resources; a variety of religions and beliefs; and creative energy.

Keller says that Christians everywhere should reach their own city in order to reach the world. The old distinction between home missions and foreign missions is made completely obsolete by today's global cities. Many remote ethnic groups, from places that Mission Marm and past missionaries viewed as mission fields, are now moving to cities.[31] Even geographically stationary people are profoundly impacted by migration, as the world is coming to them. Like the proverbial Ritz-Carlton doorman, the best-traveled man who never left his city, people now can interact with people from all over the world without leaving home.[32] In that way, Keller suggests, Christians can learn to reach major cities around the world by learning how to reach out to neighbors. Keller notes thousands of residents of New York City are far more connected to the Philippines, Haiti, Colombia, China, and Nigeria than they are to New Jersey or Connecticut.

Keller and other urban experts have observed that newcomers to major cities are also especially open to Christianity—much more so than before they left home. Having been uprooted from their traditional settings, they arrive to their new urban home at a stage of heightened openness to new ideas and change. Author Pico Iyer calls these twenty-first-century migrants and urbanites "nowherians."[33] These rootless residents experience an increasing realization of their need for help and support in order to face moral, economic, emotional, and spiritual pressures of city life, and they are receptive to others who reach out to them.

"Cities influence suburbs," Keller says, "but not vice versa." Another missions scholar agrees with Keller, noting that "the apostle Paul's strategy for spreading the gospel focused on places like Athens, Rome, Philippi, Thessalonica, and Ephesus. He saw them as gateways for the Gospel to the surrounding communities and to the travelers who passed through from distant locations. He also recognized that change and new ideas usually flow from cities to surrounding communities."[34] When urban students grow up, when urban singles get married, or when urban immigrants make money and want more space—they all move out from the city center to the suburbs. Ministries that begin and thrive in the city will eventually see their impact spread to the suburbs, following their converts out to new neighborhoods.

The Bible provides the ideal framework for helping urban dwellers deal with twenty-first-century urban syndromes like displacement, isolation, and fear. Followers of Christ must simply work to be models of community and reconciliation to strangers in their midst.

As noted by a Listening Tour participant in the massive, global city of Nairobi, Kenya, Migration has always been one of God's chosen vehicles for spreading of the gospel. The apostle Paul, Joseph, Moses, Abraham, and John the Baptist were all people on the move, and Jesus' own story was one of Migration. Today, Migration is more prominent than ever before, a Current that offers Godspeed to the church, if the church will engage it.

MIGRATION
Representative Organizations

All organizations today are influenced by Migration, but only a handful intentionally address its positive and negative impacts. Below are four excellent examples of outreaches designed for a world in which Migration is the norm.

1. **Projeto Magreb Internacional:** Projeto Magreb Internacional (PMI) is a Latin-American-based ministry that equips Spanish-speaking churches to do ministry in Muslim societies. PMI currently has over one hundred workers from more than fifteen Latin American countries, embodying the prediction that Latin America would evolve from a "mission field" into a "mission force." (www.pminternacional.org)

2. **FCS Urban Ministries:** Since 1976, FCS Urban Ministries (FCS) has focused on cities and urbanization. FCS combats urban poverty through community development programs with a focus on strengthening family relationships and creating diverse-income neighborhoods. Mainly operating in neighborhoods in Atlanta, Georgia, FCS partners with local churches to catalyze urban reinvigoration through community development initiatives like Adopt-a-Grandparent, real estate corporations, and performing arts groups. (www.fcsministries.org)

3. **E3 Partners:** E3 Partners (E3) was founded in 1987 and capitalizes on the massive increase of short-term mission trips. E3 embraces a three-part vision: equipping people for service, evangelizing, and establishing churches. With the help of fifteen thousand

international congregations and two thousand United States congregations, E3 has started twelve thousand churches throughout Argentina, Bolivia, Brazil, Colombia, Costa Rica, Ecuador, Ethiopia, India, Kenya, Panama, Peru, Romania, Russia, Rwanda, Sudan, Tanzania, Uganda, and Venezuela. E3 sends short-term mission trips to all of its target countries, with outreach ranging from sports to medicine. (www.e3partners.org)

4. **Boy Scouts of America:** For nearly a century, Boy Scouts of America (BSA) has been the largest and most prominent values-based youth development organization in the United States. While not a Christian ministry, BSA has resolutely retained its Scout Oath (in which the Scout promises "to do my duty to God and my country") in the face of boycotts, public ridicule, and withheld funds. BSA reaches out extensively to immigrants in the United States, and my son, Stefan, was the patrol leader of a Spanish-speaking start-up troop for young boys from Latin America who spoke little or no English. The adult leader of the troop in Richmond was a kindly, energetic former missionary to Latin America with the International Mission Board. (www.scouting.org)

CHAPTER 5

Monoculture

Everywhere and Nowhere

On a November morning in 2004, residents of the bustling city of Singapore awakened to a sense that something was not right. Typically oblivious to the cityscape as they sped by, the commuters in the city of 4.5 million soon saw the problem … on seven hundred bus stops around the city.

During the night, handbills had been plastered all over the city, advertising Nike's new Air Zoom LeBron II sneaker. The ads featured a graffiti-like sketch of six-foot-seven, 250-pound National Basketball Association superstar LeBron James—the very picture of force and aggression.

An outrage ensued. It wasn't that Singaporeans are repulsed by commercialism—far from it. Their per capita gross domestic product ranks twenty-fifth in the world, right behind Greece, Israel, and Germany, and miles ahead of all but a few of their geographic neighbors. The outrage wasn't because Singaporeans don't like the United States, basketball, or African-Americans, or as a whole prefer Adidas to Nike.

The reason was Singapore's famously fastidious culture. Order, conformity, and respect have been foundations of Singaporean culture for centuries. Nike knew all that and more, and admitted that the posters were intended "to disrupt the neat environment of Singapore … with the street-feel of this LeBron James basketball campaign."[1]

Just as hoped, Singaporeans reacted strongly, viewing the handbills as ugly, disrespectful, offensive, and even threatening. Employees at Clear Channel, the Singapore marketing firm that designed the campaign, said they "had a good laugh" at the response of their fellow countrymen. "It was a deliberate act, meant to give viewers the impression that some street punk had hijacked somebody else's ad campaign. It looks kind of cheeky and kind of naughty—and it got noticed," said the Singapore sales director of bus stop ads.[2]

The Nike ads had set in motion a culture clash, twenty-first-century style. The clash was highly orchestrated, rather than accidental. Nike aimed its irresistible forces of dollars and marketing straight at the immovable object of Singaporean culture. Not an isolated salvo, the campaign was the kind being staged daily by marketers around the world. Because companies profit enormously from developing expanded worldwide markets for their products and services, these in-your-face clashes are the norm, not the exception.

In Ireland, we saw Migration sweeping in and transforming the long-standing Irish culture—as well as the environment in which one Irish church planter and his congregants lived out the gospel. Similarly, in Singapore we know that followers of Christ and His church will need to adapt as the nation is changed by the fourth Global Current—*Monoculture*.

———

A global Monoculture is emerging as multinational corporations create common world tastes around logos, products, advertising slogans, stars, songs, brand names, jingles, and trademarks.[3] The Nike ad campaign is but one isolated example of an expansion-minded company pursuing global markets, in this case Asia with its huge populations, waking economies, and mounting consumerism. Furthermore, marketing campaigns like Nike's both tap into existing consumerism and cultivate more of it. Monoculture is highly flexible and adaptable, conforming to the demands of Nike and the myriad other entities that shape it, including the military and businesses, professors and press agents, religious groups and revolutionaries, gossip columnists and terrorists.

Respondents to the Listening Tour provided grassroots confirmation of Monoculture's spread. The majority of respondents noted that society in their country is changing under the influence of global media and marketing forces—and that the changes significantly affect the church's outreach efforts. They referred to the pervasive influence of the Internet, focus on pop culture, prevalence of the English language, and a common global youth culture. Many respondents also referred to increasing materialism, noting the spread of the "prosperity gospel" in the global south, where churches too often preach falsely that Christian piety translates to wealth.

While the spreading Monoculture seems normal today, it is important to recognize that it is still in its early stages. KFC signs only started popping up in China in 1987, but in 2009 there were 2,600 of the restaurants in five hundred cities, with a growth rate of one restaurant per day. Pizza Hut's first China store opened in 1990; in 2009 there were 430 Pizza Hut stores and seventy-nine delivery units in over one hundred cities in mainland China.[4] McDonald's was late on the scene, arriving in the mid-1990s. It made up for lost time, though, opening about 960 restaurants by 2008, with a plan to open 500 more stores by 2010.[5] Last in was Starbucks, which first appeared in Beijing in 1999. Nine years later, there were over 700 stores in China.[6]

As one of the world's two hundred largest corporations and one of the most recognizable brands, Nike is serious about multinational marketing.[7] Nike's aggressive ambitions have pushed the ubiquitous swoosh into retail chains, apparel, event sponsorship, stadium and arena rights, and deals with athletic leagues of all levels. It may not have been a coincidence that, two weeks before the Singapore incident, Nike signed a

100-million-dollar marketing agreement with the National Basketball Association (NBA) aimed at increasing the sport's popularity overseas, especially in Asia.[8]

Sales, costs, revenue, profit, market share—those obvious and concrete effects of business are all tracked with great regularity and precision. Much less obvious, though, are the cultural and societal impacts of marketing campaigns. When countries foster businesses and marketing, they need to know that Monoculture comes with the deal.

As a traditional Asian country, Singapore has a wary and conflicted relationship with outside influences. It seems that Singapore wishes to have its cake and eat it too (and what city or country doesn't?), by maximizing economic growth *while also* preserving indigenous cultures and traditions. City leaders clearly recognized that Monoculture, like all Global Currents, is the proverbial camel's nose under the tent: It subtly advances until it threatens cherished local ways.

The Nike flap was a case in point, with Singaporeans eventually fighting back against the perceived breach of societal cohesion, conformity, and communalism. It was by no means an exceptional case; such clashes happen throughout the world, whenever local communities rise up against Starbucks, Walmart, McDonald's, or other symbols of globalization.

The same kind of clash between outside influences and Singaporean culture had occurred, in fact, just ten years earlier in another instance of public defacement. That time, though, it escalated into an international brouhaha.

In 1994, an eighteen-year-old American student named Michael Fay was convicted on several counts of vandalism for egging and spray painting cars and stealing stop signs. A judge sentenced the Singapore American School student to four months in jail and a $2,200 fine. But what really offended Western sensibilities was that the judge ordered Fay to receive six strokes of the cane. There was not yet a twenty-four-hour news cycle at that time, but American media and diplomatic channels went on full alert, with parties from the New York Civil Liberties Union to President Clinton himself decrying the verdict and the country. Despite the public outrage and worldwide indignation, Michael Fay received his caning.[9]

Several Global Currents were at play. Migration brings more people of different backgrounds into all of our communities, and the accompanying conflict is unavoidable. Fairly or not, some insensitive and arrogant Americans affirm stereotypes of colonialism and militarism and inflame historical international resentments, one expression of the Global Current of Memory. And then, when an American corporation like Nike invades a country like Singapore, some citizens draw battle lines and rage against the machine of Monoculture.

Singapore and every country must determine how far it will go: How many traditional values will it offer up in exchange for prosperity? This kind of trade-off is a constant backdrop on today's world stage, as countries like China and India—traditional cultures—daily sacrifice culture and tradition for runaway economic growth.

Nike's campaign crossed Singapore's line—temporarily, that is—and like a rubber band that is stretched and is never as taut again, Singapore's society changed. The Air Zoom LeBron II had moved the standard. As a future-oriented company, Nike had to be especially encouraged that Singaporean kids loved the ads, many rushing to the bus stops to grab the posters as souvenirs. "It's super cool," said one fourteen-year-old—music to the ears of a company that sells "apparel as ideology."[10] Through its Singapore posters, Nike perfectly nailed its marketing sweet spot: the emerging international street and hip-hop culture, an American sports league (the NBA) sparing no cost to obtain worldwide popularity, and a twentysomething pitchman (LeBron James) who appealed to the global youth market.

The Nike ad campaign went "viral" and could not be squelched. Even if authorities pulled down posters, the buzz of the campaign helped to sell thousands of sneakers and also laid the foundation for whatever audacious ad campaign was already in the can for future release. The genie would not be stuffed back in the bottle. Nike succeeded in creating an ad campaign that sold sneakers around the world, while it also expanded the market for future sneaker sales. By ignoring cultural customs and leveling national nuances, corporations fashion markets that can be more easily targeted, accessed, and expanded. Critics—and there are many—assert that the result is "cultural strip-mining"—traditional, rich, native culture being replaced with a Monoculture of individualism, materialism, and immediacy.[11]

What does all of this have to do with the global church? A distinctive of Christianity is that Jesus inhabited our world as a full human, and He loved the earth and all of its inhabitants. He lived in a family, enjoyed beauty, endured conflict, and even worked a job. Likewise, followers of Christ are called to be in the world … but we are warned not to be *of* it. As the Current of Monoculture washes over and reshapes societies around the world, it is incumbent on the global church to muster a Christlike response. Jesus no doubt embraces Ireland and Singapore, even as they change, and He finds ways to relate to people in their environments. In that relationship, He offers another kind of transformation. How can the global church do the same in the coming years?

On May 18, 1980, in Skamania County, Washington—eight years after Nike was founded just seventy miles away—Mount St. Helens erupted. Wind-borne volcanic ash dusted the sidewalks, penthouses, public plazas, and lawns throughout the Pacific Northwest of the United States. Fifty miles from Mount St. Helens, ash piled two inches deep. Winds carried trace amounts of the ash literally around the world.

A volcanic eruption is a perfect metaphor for how Monoculture came to be. Like volcanoes, companies push ideas and images throughout the world to customers thousands of miles from the source.[12]

Once Monoculture arrives in town, the place never looks the same. Fez will look a little less like Morocco, for instance, and more like Monoculture. I saw this vividly displayed in an article in *Beyond,* Korean Air's in-flight entertainment magazine, on the way to my first visit to Korea. Its "2007 Entertainment Power List 100" helpfully instructed Koreans returning home, and visitors like me, that:

- "Nike + iPod Sport Kit will make exercise more fun, but it isn't complete without an apartment on the Han River."

- "The world is wearing Converse."

- "Che Guevara's visage is the ultimate symbol of rebellion and chic."

- "Tyra Banks speaks to the world as a star and a friend."

- "Brad and Angelina made adoption as fashionable as the designer clothes on their backs."

It is important to realize that, while Monoculture may have a strong American flavor, it is fundamentally a cultural fusion with tastes of Europe, Australia, Latin America, Asia, and more. Sometimes, national derivations become muddled and lost in the stew. Pico Iyer, a writer of Indian descent, describes being born in England, moving to California as a boy, and now dividing his time between the United States and Japan. His poignant self description as a nowherian is increasingly common:

> The country where people look like me is the one where I can't speak the language; the country where people sound like me is a place where I look highly alien, and the country where people

> live like me is the most foreign space of all. And
> though, when I was growing up, I was nearly
> always the only mongrel in my classroom or
> neighborhood, now, when I look around, there
> are more and more people in a similar state,
> the children of blurred boundaries and global
> mobility.[13]

Twenty years ago, I knew one or two nowherians; today, I know hundreds. Retaining significant differences from their upbringings, they all have now adopted common practices and features of Monoculture. The whole world watches CNN or BBC or FOX. During the Listening Tour, I saw Japanese cars on most roads I traveled. I ate Thai food on at least three continents and pizza on four. And I was surprised to see that the whole world follows the exploits of Beckham and Beyonce and Bart Simpson;[14] Freida Pinto and Tony Soprano; Yao Ming and Ronaldinho; Arsenal, Manchester United, and the Dallas Cowboys; George Clooney and Wayne Rooney; and always, heaven help us, *Baywatch*. In the end, though, the strongest undercurrent in Monoculture may just be the English language.

When I travel around the world, I use my jogs to explore cities and towns I visit. On my second day in Amman, Jordan, I went for an afternoon run, heading down a long, narrow stone stairpath toward Old Amman. As I wound farther from my business hotel, I saw fewer cars, more robes and head coverings, and eventually no Westerners. The smells were unfamiliar as I passed the stalls with lamb and goat being sliced from huge skewered hunks.

I carefully jogged down the uneven steps, winding down toward a valley neighborhood, away from the commercial district. From time to time, a little kid would jog alongside me, yelling out words that I hoped were friendly. As I rounded the corner and the valley opened up below me, I noticed that it was getting darker and the footing more difficult.

I jumped slightly at the sudden blaring, amplified muezzin's call to prayer from the block-away mosque. The broadcast cacophony (or so it sounded to my Western ears) pierced the dusk and reverberated throughout the stone streets and walls. In the midst of all the smells and sights, it was a sound that put my whole mind and body on alert, causing my heart to race and my pace to quicken.

While the call was exotic and fascinating, it was also jarring to me. It was the aural equivalent of the first time I stood on Red Square, with St. Basil's Cathedral at the far end and Lenin's Tomb and the Kremlin on my right. The huge plaza looked exactly like those grainy black-and-white newsreels of my childhood. I'd seen the May Day parades with Cold War missiles and tanks and the Red Army goose-stepping just where I now stood. In both cases—Moscow and Amman—I was right in the middle of a culture and belief system that were both foreign to me and consistently portrayed in America as a threat to me and mine. The wail went on, lasting ten or more minutes and seeming to mount in urgency and passion. By then, I found myself sprinting back to the Western familiarity of my hotel.

As I made my way back up the hill, the sidewalk narrowed. I saw her before she saw me, as she rounded the corner in a hijab, the Muslim head covering, with her eyes cast down. The path had become very narrow, and I had to turn sideways to avoid forcing her into the jagged stone wall. Not wanting to alarm her or plow into her and set off some anti-U.S. tirade or mob scene, I raised my hands together in front of my chin in the Hindu "namaste" praying position. I wasn't in India, and obviously neither she nor I was Hindu, so it was a stupid and potentially offensive, if well-meaning, gesture. But in my panic I somehow concluded that was the best way to signal that I had come in peace. I caught a glimpse of her dark, hooded eyes as they darted up at me from the rectangular cutout in her black head covering.

And then, her eyes opened wide and she flashed a smile, reassuring me in heavily accented English, "No problem. Don't worry about it."

What a jolt—from visions of death by stoning to a graphic reminder of the pervasiveness of the English language in all parts of the world! Hearing her speak English reminded me of the power of Monoculture; in this instance, it helped to dispel my fear and to signal affinity.

The world has a love-hate relationship with the United States. It hates our politics and our swagger, but how it loves our media, consumer culture, conveniences, celebrities … and the language we share with a few other countries. In a world where speaking English is often a ticket to opportunity, the global church will see great opportunities in coming years.

In China, the government has gone on record as promising that, in the future, every child will be fluent in English before finishing high school. This plan will require an estimated one million English teachers, so English-speaking Christians can expect unprecedented entrées to formerly closed areas.[15] In every country where we conducted the Listening Tour, respondents were quick to note the demand for English language skills. One respondent noted, "English is the dominant language of everything from the Internet to many wealthy Western churches, so it is important in many parts of life, including ministry."

By 2010, two billion people will speak English. Chinese, Hindi, and Arabic are among the four most-used languages in the world, their popularity due to large numbers of people for whom it is a first language. English, however, is most popular because of the huge numbers of people who learn it as a second language. More people are learning English in China today than all of the North Americans who speak English.[16]

According to BBC commentator Lord Alan Watson, "It's gone from the language of two small islands to a global working language." Commerce was an early reason to spread English colonies around the world, and English prevails partly because it easily absorbs words from other languages. According to Watson, the adoption of new words now occurs with lightning speed, thanks to global communication.[17] The great German chancellor Otto von Bismarck, as he lay dying in July 1898, was asked by a journalist what he took to be the decisive factor in then-recent history. He answered "the fact that Americans speak English."[18]

Some experts portray the continued predominance of English as inevitable.

> English has always been the dominant medium for international trade in books, records, software, and travel arrangements. But now those transactions aren't conducted just by distributors, retailers, and travel agents, but by individuals, who consequently find themselves using English to buy things that they used to buy using their local vernacular. And there is a similar effect in science, where English is increasingly being used not just in its traditional role as the language of published research but also in informal Internet discussions of methodology, professional gossip, or theoretical speculation—the sorts of topics that used to be reserved for face-to-face conversations in the lab or lunchroom, conducted in whatever the local language happened to be. In the worlds of print and broadcast, it's only the English language media—more specifically, the American media—that have been able to achieve anything like genuine worldwide news distribution.[19]

Followers of Christ have long found common ground with people of different nationalities because of the world's insatiable appetite for English language instruction. Today, the English language is one of the most dominant characteristics of Monoculture. The president of a seminary in Croatia told me about an alumnus who revisited his campus several years after graduating. The grateful young church leader thanked him profusely, saying, "You made me a man of the Word, but you also made me a man of the world, because you taught me English."[20]

I see media as a primary accomplice to Monoculture. I have watched in disgust as Monoculture spreads the Madison Avenue image of beauty around the world, causing women to feel shame about not being able to fit into a size two or four dress. In my own life, I can see how Monoculture's continuous televised coverage of wars and crises has desensitized me to violence and hatred. I also fight a distressing superficiality, as I find myself numbly watching breathless coverage of Angelina's babies, Posh's latest do, Gwyneth's children, Madonna's or Maradona's struggles. Even far removed from my modernized trappings, I have seen Monoculture's reach. I visited not one but several thatched huts in Africa with precious little furnishings or decorations … except a banner or poster of a favorite Premier League soccer team hanging on the mud wall. As the saying goes, Monoculture may not yet have reached the ends of the earth, but it can see the end from there.

Ever stuck between two streams as it lives and loves in a world of Monoculture, the global church today must be both a prophetic protester and an opportunistic creator. Presenting a distinctive and winsome witness amid Monoculture is terribly hard today, but being salt and light has never been easy. While one part of the Old Testament shows the prophet Amos railing against corporate greed and abuse, another describes Joseph in the Pharoah's court teaching young Egyptians from their own culture's "dream books."[21] As then, we must look for God's help and exhibit his grace.

In that vein, the global church should recognize, celebrate, and cultivate Monoculture's central role in shaping the Mercy Generation's social conscience. Like all Global Currents, Monoculture has rich potential for good. Instantaneous and ceaseless media coverage exposes all of us to poverty and oppression around the world, and those "touches" change many people. Global citizens today, especially youth, are compelled and impassioned to respond to the needs of the world. Once again, we see two Global Currents—Mercy and Mutuality—propelling each other and able to propel (or stall) the church.

In February 2006, a start-up ministry called To Write Love on Her Arms (TWLOHA) hit the Global Current sweet spot: It is a Mercy Generation ministry orchestrating and drawing upon the very latest Machines like MySpace, Facebook, Twitter, and YouTube. It tapped into the global Monoculture through popular rock bands and spread virally through the global youth culture over the Internet.

Like all Machines, the Internet is flexible and malleable, effective for conveying messages good or bad. TWLOHA capitalized on the viral nature of Monoculture and did an end run around "old media" tools like advertising, direct mail solicitations, brochures, public-service announcements on radio and television, etc. In the process, the ministry also saved large amounts of money.

TWLOHA began when a group of young men decided to help a friend pay for drug treatment by selling T-shirts with the phrase "To Write Love on Her Arms." They gained attention and growing popularity, fueled by celebrity endorsements by the bands Anberlin and Switchfoot. TWLOHA's founders created a functional and compelling Web site, and their primary theme was their strong belief in the message of hope. With 336,146 friends on MySpace, 24,148 followers on Twitter, a strong presence on YouTube, and over 100 groups on Facebook—the largest group (their fan page) having 165,231 fans—TWLOHA shows how Monoculture can edify and enhance society.

As I serve my role in the global church and look beyond the Meeting of the Waters, my heart and mind draw me to work within Monoculture and not to bemoan it. The Global Currents move relentlessly and virally, and trying to stop them is not my particular role. Rather, I urge fellow followers of Christ to join me in discerning how to use Monoculture for God's good and our own.

For several reasons, a disproportionate number of young adults and youth shape Monoculture. Sheer demographics are the most straightforward reason, as seen in the projection that 65 percent of all Africans will be sixteen years of age or less by the year 2010.

Secondly, those young adults and youth are effective and cheap ambassadors within their own circles. Many of the Singaporean youth who saw the LeBron James posters went on to buy Nike sneakers; others tore down posters to tape in their homes or show to friends, agents of further Air Zoom dissemination like a jet stream carrying volcanic fallout one more mile out from its source.

Youth and young adults—that sixteen- to twenty-five-year-old demographic coveted and courted by marketers worldwide—are heavily influenced by the Internet, television, and other tools that corporations and media wield so effectively. Messages borne by Monoculture often reach their young adult target immediately and persuasively. The very best example is MTV, for no modern media outlet has disseminated its brand, message, and lifestyle more effectively.

> [T]he international church ... has some new competitors that are rarely mentioned at evangelical missions conferences. Those who are doing a brilliant job at world "evangelization" are the marketers of McWorld. Two Pentecostal pastors ... reported that in the previous five years they had both lost their entire youth groups. When I asked how that happened, they

explained that five years ago, American MTV came to town and had a major influence in the lives of their youth that they hadn't found a way to contend with. In the last fifteen years we have witnessed the creation of something we have never seen before: a borderless global youth culture. Everywhere we travel we find young people wearing the same jeans, drinking the same soda and hard-wired into the same American pop-consumer culture.[22]

There is, indeed, a global youth culture. Singaporean youth today often have more in common with youth in Sydney, Shanghai, and São Paolo than with their parents or even Singaporean youth of a decade ago. Here, too, we see the Global Currents intertwining and reinforcing one another: The global youth culture, which is such a strong contributor to Monoculture, is fed and accelerated by urbanization and Migration, which carry cultures and trends from one city to another.

So I was not really surprised during a 2004 trip to Havana, Cuba, to see that the global youth culture is even making inroads in that closed-off Communist island. It all started in a meeting with a group of about ten elderly pastors in the kitchen of a local church. Religion in twenty-first-century Cuba is opaque, more a matter of Russian roulette than rule of law. It was very moving to hear the pastors' stories of commitment and courage in the face of torture, detention, and threat. After we had been talking awhile, I asked those fiercely resilient men how bad the Revolution had been. They reflected back to January 1959, when a tiny band of revolutionaries led by Fidel Castro, his brother Raul, and Che Guevara marched from the Sierra Maestra mountains into Havana, sending General Fulgencia Batista fleeing to the Dominican Republic. Their eyes filled with tears as, one after another, they told me about the harsh repression in those early days. By comparison, the government's more recent posture of disdain and neglect toward religion was a gift from God.

Wondering about the impact of the global youth culture, I asked the pastors if they employed any special approaches to teach youth about Christianity. They responded with blank stares, agreeing that no particular efforts were needed to reach youth; all children would learn about faith just like they always had, through "la familia."

My boyhood best friend was a Cuban refugee named Tony Fidel Perez, and many days at his house taught me that families and extended relatives are focal points of Latin American life. I got that. The tradition-minded, white-haired pastors I spoke to simply assumed that things would remain the same within their churches and families.

But church leaders around the world, through the Listening Tour, had overwhelmingly pointed to changes in younger generations which, in turn, they saw profoundly affecting society, public life, family, and the church:

- "The influence of globalization has really infiltrated youth."

- "The children are exposed to so much more than before, and they don't have the tools to handle it."

- "My son likes Pepsi and McDonald's. I like coconut and tea shops.… I call it 'Pepsi Culture.' Even the church is facing this 'McDonaldization.' It's an instant culture."

- One person noted that the influence of the global media and the Internet have connected youth and teens, popularizing the same things worldwide, from similar bands, sports stars, and clothing to praise songs and Christian authors.

- "We are worried. For three or four generations of evangelicals, there have been threats from outside the church.... Young generations are losing their identity. Television, markets, sexuality, and 'New Age' religions are making it really difficult to figure out truth."

For years, I had observed the global youth culture around the world with my own eyes, and I learned about it further from the Listening Tour. Though I respected the trust of the venerable pastors in tradition and families, I suspected that a global youth culture was probably present in Cuba, even if it had not yet surfaced in their line of sight. An important benefit of charting the Global Currents is helping such leaders to recognize changes bubbling up around local churches, even when those changes are not yet immediately apparent or forceful.

Later that same day, the mission group I was visiting took us to sixteenth-century Fort Morro, built on a spit in Havana Bay across from Old Havana's crumbling seafront villas. As Atlantic waves crashed on the rocks and palm trees rustled in the tropical breeze, throngs of Cuban teens draped themselves on the fort's walls, benches, and the huge old cannons that had fought off British expeditions.

For an hour or so, our small klatch of Americans wound its way through the dense crowds and finally crossed the moat, going out the gates of the castle. I sidled up to Pastor Mike, a San Diego megachurch pastor who was one of my favorite traveling companions because of his fun-loving nature and spiritual depth. So I was surprised by his downcast demeanor as we made our way out of Fort Morro.

Mike told me he was distressed by the empty and agitated youth we had just seen. He said he had sensed a palpable restlessness and anger in the youth. Mike worked extensively with gangs and juvenile offenders in the United States, and he observed similar troubling indicators among the Cuban youth. As we strolled, we talked about possible causes of their unrest. From an economic perspective, we know youth in poorer countries are often embittered at the pervasive grinding poverty, especially when coupled with an utter lack of prospects for future improvement. Politically, Cuba's internal and international relations were newly volatile after decades of oppressive stability. That gave some cause for hope, but in the recent past hope had always been a bitter opening act for disappointment. And spiritually, Cuban youth raised in a Communist society had too rarely experienced personal, life-giving exposure to Jesus Christ.

There were also some external reasons for unrest in Cuba. After a half century of being closed off from many global forces, Cuba had trace amounts of Monoculture. Cuba's tattered and tired Communist ideology had withstood countless economic, military, and political incursions; these days, though, resourceful and law-breaking Cubans are opening the floodgates to a constant stream of television shows and movies and music and news. The nation is no longer completely closed. Like volcanic ash, traveling over, around, and through the official filters and censors, Monoculture has introduced itself to the island.

All told, Cuban youth today have good reasons to feel lost and angry—reasons that deserve to be heard and considered. The pastors I met—godly, faithful, and effective for the long haul—may well be looking more to the past than the future. Their distinctive Cuban culture will surely become more like the Monoculture … and I pray that they will not be the last to know. There are, after all, years of wonderfully challenging and fulfilling ministry awaiting followers of Christ living in Monoculture.

The Bible promises—and history confirms—that close encounters with the lived-out gospel will be attractive and compelling. Wherever Monoculture advances in the form of the global youth culture, the global church should also expect that opportunities will abound for creative, relevant, authentic Christian witness. Further, the church should celebrate that youth who are newly exposed to the gospel—in Cuba, in former Soviet countries, and in post-Christian countries with little current Christian influence—have not been inoculated against Jesus Christ. Christianity has been, during their young lives, a non-factor. A pastor planting churches in Amsterdam told me that youth in his city are invariably open to authentic, relational Christianity, if not to formal, tradition-bound Christian churches. Sounds like what Jesus encountered—and took advantage of—in His days on earth.

MONOCULTURE
Representative Organizations

Societies around the world must adapt as media, technology, and immigration create a global Monoculture. Liberalized economies, individualism, feminism, and a global youth culture all have positive effects, but they also present deep problems. Below are four ministries that recognize Monoculture and equip believers to be salt and light—winsome, distinctive, and positive.

1. **Crown Financial Ministries:** Since 1976, Crown Financial Ministries (CFM) has equipped people to learn, apply, and teach biblical financial principles. An interdenominational ministry, CFM has taught or equipped more than 50 million people in over eighty nations with the life-transforming message of faithfully living by God's financial principles in every area of their lives. (www.crown.org)

2. **Damaris Project:** The Damaris Project was founded in 1997 to help women convene and converse about femininity and spirituality. Lilian Calles Barger, the Damaris Project's founder, wrote the book *Eve's Revenge: Women and a Spirituality of the Body* to address the disconnect between women's bodies and souls in today's media-soaked culture. The Damaris Project is a bare-bones group based in Dallas, Texas, and is run completely by volunteers, with 95 percent of its funding coming from small donations, often online. (http://damarisproject.org)

3. **Integra Russia:** Two Slovakian business partners founded Integra in 1995 with a vision to encourage the establishment of businesses based on integrity. Integra provides training and other forms of support in

Slovakia, Romania, Bulgaria, Russia, Croatia, Serbia, Kenya, Sudan, and the United States. (http://integrarussia.ru/en/index.htm)

4. **To Write Love on Her Arms:** Begun in 2006 as a MySpace page, TWLOHA is a nonprofit that uses the Internet to encourage people who are victims of depression, addiction, or self-injury or who are contemplating suicide to seek help and embrace hope. TWLOHA's Web site has a twofold purpose: to serve as a bridge to telephone help lines and to answer posted messages from people around the world. In its first two years, TWLOHA responded to over eighty thousand online messages in forty countries. (www.twloha.com)

CHAPTER 6

Machines

Both Jekyll and Hyde

"A little breeze whipped up at five p.m.," said the man from Bogalay, Burma, "and at eight the rain began, and then at ten the sky turned bright red." Incredulous, I pressed him through our translator—"The sky was *bright red ... at night?* Do you mean like that color?"—pointing to a blood-red poster. "Yes," he said, then stared blankly at the floor in front of him, as the memories flooded back.

"There had been some rumors about a storm that night," he continued, "but people got over it. In Burma we are accustomed to severe weather, especially as the rainy season approaches." Few Burmese knew, though, that a meteorological nightmare was heading their way. It had been originally projected to strike southeastern India, but instead took a right-hand turn and picked up speed somewhere over the Indian Ocean, transforming into a deadly Category 4 cyclone.

Cyclone Nargis was at peak force when it slammed into Burma (now officially called Myanmar[1]) on May 2, 2008. Winds up to 135 miles per hour created a tidal surge at the exact location where it would inflict the most damage: at the Irrawaddy Delta with its sparse protective vegetation, heavily populated villages, and extended families living in flimsy shacks on farms just above sea level. A wall of water twelve feet high swept over hundreds of villages as far as twenty-five miles inland. Right in Nargis's path at the mouth of a river, Bogalay lost 10,000 of its 190,000 residents and 95 percent of its homes in that one horrific night. That's more than three times the death toll of the World Trade Center attack, in one small city, in one dark night.

One Bogalay resident recounted his nightmare experience: "At first I saw four dead bodies and was shocked and scared. I had never seen a corpse before. Then, I saw hundreds of bodies." Another resident lived in one of the few structures that survived in Bogalay and recalled the waters surging underneath his stilted house. His face contorted in grief as he recalled the "thwack, thwack" of corpses carried by the rushing current and slamming into the stilts and floorboards beneath the house.

Nargis was one of the world's deadliest natural disasters of all time, possibly far worse than the 2004 tsunami … but no one knows for sure. The secretive Burmese government simply stopped counting deaths at 146,000 in order to minimize political fallout.[2] Several leading international relief agencies acknowledged that official estimates might be grossly conservative. As news leaked out, disaster-relief organizations from around the world readied to mobilize their resources into the Nargis-affected area. To the international community's horror, though, the Burmese government did not accept outside help for more than a week while hunger, disease, trauma, and dead bodies mounted. One foreign relief worker, who arrived at the Irrawaddy Delta as soon as the Burmese junta allowed, told me "everyone knows the death figure might really be more than one million."

A world of humanitarian relief could have been on its way to Burma, even as soon as that red sky was turning to dawn. International relief experts had already begun their projections of victim counts and damage tolls, volunteers and professionals were planning their flights, supplies were being inventoried and loaded, and logistics finalized—all just waiting for the word to go.

The offers of international support poured in, as is often the case in the aftermath of such massive and deep suffering. When the nongovernment organizations (NGOs) finally flooded into Burma's delta ten days later, the world sighed in relief. The fact that the government had kept willing help at bay for over a week while the cyclone's aftermath continued to claim victims, though, made Nargis a double disaster.

The governmental straight-arm was especially frustrating because seasoned relief workers tell me that NGOs today have the ability to respond to disasters with levels of information, speed, and success unthinkable just a decade ago. Nargis was a powerful lesson, both about how quickly twenty-first-century relief agencies can swing into action and about what can happen when they don't.

One relief expert after another told me about the innovations transforming the fields of relief, development, and disaster response. This is very good news indeed for future victims—and for the global church that will surely serve them. Disaster relief in the future will be more sustainable, rapid, efficient, accountable, and humane, all because of the tide of the fifth Global Current—*Machines*.

Almost a year after Nargis, a journalist visiting the Burmese capital of Yangon (formerly called Rangoon) wrote that it "looks pretty much back to normal—for a city of the last century, at least."[3] The wealthiest country in Southeast Asia until 1960, Burma is now poor and emasculated because of generations of repressive rule.[4] As I strolled through the streets, Yangon seemed backward and stuck in time, between the distinctive clay-smeared Burmese cheeks to protect against the tropical sun, the curbside vendors selling fresh seafood cooked over open fires, the old men sitting at sidewalk tea shops playing checkers, the street cleaners sweeping sidewalks with rustic thatch brooms, and the gutters flowing with I-didn't-want-to-know-what. I suppose it is a good thing that the Burmese people are generally peaceful and passive, with minimal expectations for income, social services, or government responsiveness of any kind.

Knowing that I had an unusual opportunity, as a foreigner, to visit the Irrawaddy Delta, I studied all of the published statistics about Nargis's toll. I was especially eager to see how the delta was recovering and how outsiders were helping with that process. I wanted to witness and learn how the global church had served—and *should* serve—communities in places like post-Nargis Burma.

I am convinced that when I go to heaven, the last leg of my trip will be a van ride. I cannot count the number of times I have left my hotel at daybreak to sit on barely-cushioned bench seats for half-day rides to remote sites—in Uganda, Serbia, Brazil, China, Russia, Guatemala, India, Cuba, North Korea, South Africa, Jordan, Morocco, and so many more countries. On that particular February morning, I was driven six hours southeast from the sprawling, bustling chaos of Yangon, through the remote countryside, and then into the populous, flat delta region, which is where Nargis did its damage.

As the van hurtled from highways to dirt roads to rocky lanes, Burma's countryside flashed by—neon-green rice paddies, sun-drenched dirt fields, roof-high sunflowers, palm groves. The people were ever friendly, waving as our van maneuvered around them—barefooted men walking alongside and switching their water buffalo, field-workers in those conical bamboo hats, children rolling hoops or tires with sticks, men poling flat-bottom canoes down canals and rivers. And everywhere, the Buddhists in their ox-blood red robes.

The people in delta villages appeared to be busy reconstructing their lives as fishermen, farmers, net weavers, seamstresses, cooks, or repairmen. Nargis brought most Delta livelihoods to a standstill: 63 percent of the land in the most-affected villages was inundated with salt water; more than

700,000 tons of milled rice stored for export and local consumption were ruined; 50 percent of buffalo were killed; and 100,000 fishing boats were damaged or destroyed.[5]

Rather than just meeting emergency needs and then moving on, many relief organizations were thankfully still on-site when I visited the Irrawaddy Delta in early 2009. Though many of the NGOs were Christian, Burmese law forbade them from expressing their faith overtly, at the risk of having their humanitarian visas revoked and their Burmese staff members hassled, prosecuted, or worse. Instead, the NGOs focused on material needs of the residents, such as helping farmers prepare for the first planting season, distributing water filters, constructing pit latrines, and providing medical supplies. To help revive the devastated economy, NGOs donated threshing machines, hand tractors, fishing boats, threads for weaving nets, and livestock. I marveled at how many of the organizations' responses, even nine months after the cyclone, continued to be mechanical and technological.

After the van ride mercifully ended, we boated several hours down the Bogalay River. We docked at a Buddhist school and left our shoes in the boat so that we could walk up the boardwalk and enter the sacred temple. There we met the gentle, smiling head monk whose school was collaborating with Christian NGOs to provide education, playgrounds, health care, and water distribution centers for all villagers whose homes were destroyed.

We then motored on to another school, where a boy told us about watching his parents and siblings swept out to sea by the storm surge as he clung to a tree. He quietly admitted that he still cries when he thinks about his family, and a doting grandfather draped an arm around the small boy. While children at the other two schools screamed and squealed happily on a playground built by an international NGO, the children at this school seemed serious and stoical. Consistent with my perceptions of Burmese people as placid and resilient, I will never forget this brave-but-broken boy.

When I think of him, I remember that Cyclone Nargis only lasted one night, but its effects will be felt for generations. The global church needs to know that too.

———————

As a child, I remember fishing change out of my pocket to drop in the coin hole in the little cardboard box for earthquake or flood or famine drives. Even then, I knew that Christ calls His church to serve the orphans and widows and to provide water and clothing for the poor. I always thought the boxes were cool, because they started as flattened cardboard sheets, with tabs and slots so that you could carefully assemble them and go and do your part to help. The coins, or donated clothing or canned goods, were about as close as a boy in New Jersey could get to participating in what was happening in Biafra, Bangladesh, Guatemala, or India. I am not sure where the collected coins were taken, or how long it took for them to get to the disaster region.

Today, I sit at my desk in Richmond, and once again I am thinking about a natural disaster on the other side of the world. This time, though, I am looking at before-and-after photos of the Irrawaddy Delta, taken by Moderate Resolution Imaging Spectroradiometer (MODIS) on NASA's Terra satellite.[6] MODIS used visible and infrared light to show the extent and location of Nargis's flooding in two color images, the first from April 15, 2008, and the other from May 5, 2008, three days after Nargis. Even to my untrained eye, the first photograph shows sharply defined rivers and lakes against a backdrop of green vegetation and brown patches. In the May 5 photo, the entire coastal plain is covered with water. Fallow land appears to have been hit especially hard, probably because of a lack of vegetation to slow the flooding. Yangon, one hundred miles from the Delta, is completely surrounded by floods, and muddy runoff colors the coastal areas. These images and more were immediately available to relief organizations after Nargis's landfall.

"How is it possible that there was such a great death toll in the twenty-first century when we have imagery from satellites in real time and there are specialized meteorology centers in all the regions?" wondered an official with the United Nations.[7] There are two answers, and both have to do with Machines.

First, Burma suffered from a lack of emergency infrastructure. According to the World Meteorological Organization, Burma is different from neighboring Bangladesh and India because it has no radar network to predict the location and height of storm surges. Bangladesh has a storm protection system that includes warning sirens, evacuation routes, and sturdy towers to shelter people. Sirens are rudimentary Machines, but even they were lacking in Burma. Experts are certain that Nargis's death toll would have been dramatically lower if Burma had such basic systems in place.[8]

Second, the Burmese government closed off all information and access to the disaster site for ten days after Nargis's landfall.[9] I have since learned of an amazing array of technology available to meet disaster-related needs, none of which were allowed during the run-up and aftermath of Cyclone Nargis.

I wanted to talk with an expert about how Machines can aid disaster-relief efforts in the twenty-first century, and a chain of referrals led me to Brian Carlson. Brian is an eleven-year veteran with World Vision International, where he serves as the Humanitarian and Emergency Affairs Information Technology (IT) Director. World Vision is a Christian international relief and development organization with over thirty-three thousand staff in ninety-seven countries, impacting one hundred million individuals every year. The world's largest nonprofit NGO, World Vision addressed more than seventy-five humanitarian emergencies around the world in 2008, including a massive earthquake in China, flooding in India, and Cyclone Nargis.[10] Brian told me that, for disasters like Nargis, Machines are absolutely essential to effective relief work.

"The biggest developments today are in the field of early warning," he said. "We are currently working with NASA, Google, Cisco, Microsoft, and other high-tech companies to do scenario planning. When disasters like cyclones occur, we can know within certain distances where the cyclone will hit, the population density, where roads are, which bridges are at high risk for being washed out, what types of agriculture and crops are endangered, and the locations of infrastructure like hospitals, fire, and police … if there are any."

I asked Brian how relief organizations like World Vision obtain all of that village- and region-specific information, and he cited a technology I often heard referenced by my many sources—Geographic Information Systems (GIS). "Through GIS satellite technology we can place data in its geographic context with geographic coordinates. As a disaster approaches, we have the information to build warehouses outside of the anticipated devastation zone with pre-positioned goods that will be needed—food, fabric, medications, and temporary shelters. Workers use remote sensing data for situation analysis, tracking how well equipment, food, supplies, and personnel are dispersed to places of greatest need. Also, we anticipate the skill sets that will be needed in different areas, such as agricultural experts, counselors, water experts, or doctors."

I once attended a conference where two State Department officials spoke about "scenario planning," but I had never considered it in the context of Christian ministry. I soon realized, though, that what Brian described was exactly how the global church should navigate: downstream from the Meeting of the Waters.

- The approach utilizes relief workers (most of them indigenous) who were already on the ground making intensive investments in the faiths and lives of local people. Mission Marm would approve of this.

- The approach utilizes Machines to deliver relief services better—quicker, to more people, and in greater collaboration. That is just the way Apple Guy would do it.

- The innovative use of Machines combines best practices and data from information technology, meteorology, relief and development, sociology and anthropology, theology and missiology. This, of course, is the epitome of information arbitrage as described by Thomas Friedman.

I asked Brian one last question, "During the technology revolution of the past eleven years, what have been the biggest changes in the use of Machines for relief work?" He did not need to think for long: "Our best practices are so much more advanced than they used to be. When I started, we would go into disaster situations with pen and pencil. That is how we would capture data on infant mortality, malaria, diarrhea, vaccinations, clean water, sanitation, life expectancy, and more. Now we use handheld GIS devices to 'geotag' information. When field workers install a well," he said, "they take a picture of it and text the information to a central source, such as Google Maps. That way, a community in a remote area can map its water infrastructure, and people all around can now know where to get clean water."

World Vision and other leading relief and development organizations devote enormous resources to training local people to maintain the Machines that are installed. In the past, lack of sustainability has been a huge black mark on the efforts of many aid programs. Developing nations are littered, for instance, with recently installed water wells that are dry—inoperative because of lack of simple maintenance. One relief agency head told me, "The technology is the smallest piece of the pie when it comes to relief and development work. The biggest challenge is management technology—the ways and processes for transferring the technology to the community."[11]

Brian continued, "Field workers can also do data collection through cell phones, for instance, tracking the number of deposits into microfinance institutions, assessing the success of water and sanitation intervention, tracking disease and epidemics, and more. We've been able to go from having missionary-type IT shops to professional IT shops comparable with any Fortune 500 company." In other words, World Vision has capitalized on Mission Marm's investment in indigenous people and introduced Apple Guy's tools and toys—all to the end of loving neighbors and spreading good news.

Followers of Christ obey two major biblical mandates: the Great Commandment and the Great Commission. The Great Commandment instructs us to love the Lord wholly and also to love our neighbors as ourselves.[12] World Vision's staff serves victims without regard for religious affiliation, but it is clearly Jesus' example and leading that draws workers like Brian to places like Bogalay.

In the Great Commission, Jesus told His followers to make disciples in all the world.[13] Ever since, world evangelization has been a central and abiding value of the global church. Not surprisingly, evangelization-minded ministries have tapped into the power of computers. One mission researcher noted, "Computers are enormously flexible tools, as adaptable as they are powerful. As ministry perspectives have moved, computer applications have also moved."[14] In other words, computers can help to feed and clothe—and save—people around the world.

Using computers for evangelism may offend some Christians who see "sharing the gospel" as an inherently personal act best done in life-on-life, person-to-person settings. The idea of making evangelism "scalable" (a common business and computer concept meaning expandable) through technology is anathema to some. Over the centuries, though, many Machines have emerged which made evangelism more scalable:

- Books and tracts made biblical content accessible to the masses.

- Voice amplification through loudspeakers birthed mass rallies and campaigns.

- Radio broadcasting allowed Bible programming to be distributed to the world's most remote countries, regions, and villages.

- Movies provided a powerful vehicle for Christian messages.

- Television was cost-effective and intimate.

Today, the Machines changing the landscape and horizons of Christian evangelization are computers, in ever-new ways. And, at the beginning, it *did* take rocket scientists to push world evangelization into the brave new world of computers.

Bob Waymire was a rocket engineer who left Lockheed Martin to do computer-based research on church planting at the Research and Strategy Department of One Challenge, a ministry located in Silicon Valley. David Barrett was a British aeronautical engineer and test pilot whose *Missionary Notes* (published from 1946–1960) "applied scientific and aeronautical methodologies to mission, utilizing Britain's first operational computer, the electromechanical Colossus with its 18,000 vacuum tubes and covering some 2,000 square feet of floor space."[15] Ed Dayton was an aeronautical engineer who moved to World Vision to harness computers' potential for organizing large masses of information for the task of global evangelization. Bill Dickson was an engineering student who became aware of the enormity of evangelizing millions of unreached people and concluded, "If you're dealing with thousands of anything, you've got to get a computer in there somewhere." Patrick Johnstone was a chemical-engineer-turned-evangelist who programmed a multiuser computer with a data-rich guide for praying for every country in the world, called *Operation World*. Pete Holzmann, a Stanford-educated electrical engineer and well-known *wunderkind* in the infant northern California computer industry, helped to resource and start several mission organizations.

All of those men saw rich opportunities to transform the task of global evangelization by collecting and organizing massive amounts of data for use by the global church. They captured statistics on the varieties of ethnic groups in various countries, cities, provinces, languages, and people groups. They documented the number and location of churches in regions. They tracked the availability of the Bible (including various chapters, books, or Testaments) in written form, audio form, or video. They researched population by religion, religion growth trends, and denominations within Christianity. They studied residents' ages, education levels, languages spoken, and literacy. And, they documented the presence of church-planting movements and the number of missionaries sent to and sent from that country. All of that data helped Christian workers to identify and connect better with indigenous people.

Those pioneers using computers in missions were few in number but brilliant and entrepreneurial. They also brought several cardinal commitments to their Christian callings—achieving technological excellence, collaborating with each other, and valuing the Great Commission over great potential wealth.

"I have probably helped to generate a *minimum* of one and a half billion dollars in profits for other people. I'm glad for them, because I've always seen my industry career as earning time for my ministry work, rather than earning a lot of money," Pete Holzmann told me with his inimitable crooked grin and eager response. "Leslie and I have happily used up our life's savings several times along the way. The only thing that matters is that God has me where He wants me, and I'm surrounded by people who feel the same way."

Pete reflected with me on his consuming and uneasy relationship with Machines. Because his father worked for General Electric, Pete's childhood home was one of the few in the world with a computer teletype terminal. By the time he finished high school, he had mastered a dozen programming languages.

Pete went on to study semiconductor electronics at Stanford University, where he moonlighted as a consultant to make ends meet. He quickly found himself working with world-leading experts on top projects, including the first digital telephone, the first retail microcomputer (it retailed for around one thousand dollars at Macy's), the first laser printer and desktop publishing system, and one job where he helped to make universal email communication possible among customers of different networks. "I did all this accidentally," he recalled, "out of my garage with an unlisted number. And along the way, I was the largest laptop reseller in Silicon Valley for a few years."

Pete graduated from Stanford in 1979 and recalls, "I just wanted to be a normal guy with a normal family and a normal life. But God wouldn't let me do that. I didn't want to work with computers, but those were the best jobs I could find." Pete took on consulting jobs, and found his business clients willing to pay him more and more for his time. He saw that as an opportunity to commit fewer hours to his consulting business and more to his ministry clients. "I felt burdened with gifts and skills that were not being used for God. He wanted more than a few hours per week and a few dollars; He wanted all of me." Eventually, a consulting client offered to pay his full salary and underwrite his ministry expenses in exchange for just one-quarter of his time.

During high school, Pete grew disillusioned with computers because he felt divided in that world. "Through elementary and high school, I successfully avoided oral reports," he told me with a laugh. "I was a computer whiz, but I couldn't talk to other people." He recognized that his computer skills allowed him to isolate himself, but he knew that God wanted him to be in community.

During his university years and since, he began to see that the computer world rewards analysis and facts, but that movements of the Spirit are inexplicable. Computers exist to produce results, but God wants us to rest in the process. Computers encourage self-reliance, but God calls us toward dependency.

In time, Pete said he sensed God saying, "I gave you this expertise for a reason." In 1998, Pete founded the International Christian Technologists Association (ICTA), a ministry to help fellow techies practice what he calls "Spirit-led technology." Mirroring the long, heady path Pete has traveled, ICTA's Web site refers to "an unusual perspective on information, technology, success, measurement." Echoing Pete's struggle with the divide between faith and Machines, the Web site encourages Christian technologists that their careers can be:

- "Relational, an authentic, selfless, inspiring love story";

- "Practical, industry-tested, scientific, high tech";

- "Faith-filled, leaning on God";

- "Both. And. —Seamless."

Seamless is right: Pete Holzmann brings his spiritual perspective both to the global church and to the computer field. In ICTA, he has created a Christian fellowship that nurtures brilliant technology leaders in companies around the world. In addition, in his business career ("on the side," as he put it), he has made remarkable landmark contributions to the field of information technology.

In the early 1980s, Pete was volunteering his services for an international mission agency when a missionary excitedly showed him some new computer-generated maps. He challenged Pete to generate similar maps that would further Christian evangelization around the world. Pete took on the challenge—by assembling a team that worked for years on the very ambitious project. Their first result was a 1983 map of Guatemala that showed data on evangelical Christian presence, province by province. Summarizing that improbable accomplishment, a journalist wrote:

[Pete was] the chief architect of the world's first PC-based geographic information system (GIS). This significant technological development was thus largely crafted by a gifted Christian who all along had in view its usefulness for world mission. The leading PC-based GIS software in the world today, ArcView, indirectly benefits from Holzmann's work.[16]

World Vision's Brian Carlson told me that most of the exciting technological developments in disaster relief involved GIS technology. Little did either of us know at the time that GIS technology was made accessible by Pete Holzmann, a fellow follower of Christ devoted to harnessing Machines to fulfill the Great Commission and the Great Commandment. Whenever Brian uses that GIS technology, in Burma or elsewhere, he has Pete Holzmann to thank. That idea would embarrass Pete greatly, because he is simply awed by how his life, once divided by Machines, has been so beautifully redeemed and integrated by God. Seamless indeed.

So, are there any downsides to Machines—dangerous undercurrents that might take the church off course? In this chapter, Brian Carlson approached Machines positively, using GIS and GPS to enable better disaster relief. Pete Holzmann was ambivalent toward Machines, remembering that power comes from God and not computers, but also utilizing computers powerfully to resource world evangelization.

A report by McKinsey & Company in 2006 stated, "We are at the early, not mature, stage of the technological revolution."[17] If Machines have had such a radical impact on the global church during technology's early stages, then what should we expect in the coming years?

Already a rich area of ministry, even a cursory glimpse of Internet initiatives reveals Internet evangelism, study guides, Web sites, education by extension, online communities, videos, music, Web publications, webinars, voice-over-Internet calls, movies, video games, dating services, online devotionals, and much more. In addition, brand-new technologies develop daily.

As the global church considers the increasing opportunities presented by the Internet, it must decide, as with any of the Global Currents: ride it or resist it? Well, there are indeed Christians advocating restraint.

Speaking about social networking, for instance, author Shane Hipps voices strong reason to *resist* it: "I find it troubling that so many communities of faith are in hot pursuit of these technologies. The Internet is seen as the Holy Grail of 'building community.' However, churches will find the unintended consequences of this medium coming back to bite them. The Internet is a lot of things, but it is emphatically *not* a neutral aid."[18]

Pete Holzmann, the ambivalent computer whiz, also offers strong concerns. With the greatly expanded memories of computers, he says, "Conversations are no longer temporary. Something someone writes is preserved, and twenty years later it's all online. The problem is that there is no grace when conversations are permanent. That generates tremendous baggage."

David Dose also sees the dark side of Machines—in fact, he *lives* there.

I first met David about three years ago at a private meeting of international ministry people in a rural setting. Mid-presentation, the windowless room went pitch black, and a group of men burst in the back door, ordering us to lie face down on the ground. About six of them barged in, fired a few shots in the air, scuffled with some group members, and then rushed out as quickly as they came. After a few minutes in dark silence, those of us on the floor gathered ourselves and began to peek around. It turned out that two of the people in the meeting—I did not know either of them—were missing. Before too long, ministry leaders were contacted and received a video of the two Christian workers who were being held as hostages. The video showed the very nervous blindfolded man and woman, who assured us that they were fine, obviously aware that a verbal slip could cost lives—theirs and others.

As we watched the video, David Dose helped us to analyze the situation and assess how well the hostages were handling the interrogation. Were they providing plausible information, even if they were not telling everything they knew? Were they giving out enough information to placate their captors but not enough to put their colleagues or indigenous believers at risk? Were they striking the right balance between friendliness and defiance? How could they draw strength from God in a situation like that?

David Dose, thank God, had masterminded the whole simulated event. The kidnappers were actually his employees at Fort Sherman Academy, a privately owned Idaho business that he founded to provide security training to missionaries, charitable aid groups, government employees, the military, and business people. The mission agency that convened the conference had invited Fort Sherman to their missionary conference in a rural east coast venue to train its workers to anticipate, recognize, and survive what Dose euphemistically called "contingency situations."

Dose is a Department of Defense-trained expert in high-risk hostage survival techniques and was a government counterterrorism instructor for eleven years. Fort Sherman has over fifty full- and part-time personnel, works with seventy-five organizations in thirty countries worldwide, and currently trains approximately three thousand individuals annually in varied settings.

The stakes are enormously high in the repressive countries where so many missionaries work. In places like Saudi Arabia, much of central Asia, and North Africa, Christians constantly labor under the threat of being detained for interrogation, being evicted from the country, or seeing communities of indigenous Christians put at risk of persecution or even death. For David Dose, success is measured in tragedies avoided, and he emphasizes that doing everything right can still result in casualties. Terrorism is not predictable, logical, or by the book. The Fort Sherman Web site acknowledges the risks: "To date, we have had the privilege of training over 16,000 civilians worldwide in courses varying from 1 to 11 days—depending on the level of training required. And to date, we have had 62 of our graduates endure a kidnapping, illegal detention, carjacking, home invasion, or other violent crime in the course of their work or travel overseas. As of now, 61 of those graduates are alive and free." I was alarmed by the stark reference to casualties, but David pointed out that Fort Sherman's survival record was significantly above the 80 percent national average for similar types of incidents in foreign settings.[19]

"When we provide contingency training for mission agencies," Dose told me, "our goal is a more unified response that will be more pleasing to Christ. That includes how to respond to each other, to family, to the media, to victims' needs, to nonbelievers and nationals on the ground. How they function when lives are at stake is an opportunity to model the gospel. They may even expand their ministry by people seeing them respond that way in crisis situations.

"We spend most of our time training international workers about how to recognize when they are in danger and how to defend against it. And today, the technology that is part of missionaries' everyday lives is putting the global church at great risk. Terrorists are now using technology to commit crimes against foreign targets, like missionaries, in ways they couldn't previously have done because of cost."

I told David a pet theory of mine: "International Christian workers are the world's *most* dependent people on their Machines. As they travel, their cell phones, BlackBerrys, iPhones, laptops, and memory sticks are umbilical cords to the lives they left behind—their families, colleagues, churches, committees, reading, research, and writing. Machines allow Christian workers to maintain their life ties as they travel through airports, hotels, the outback, and the bush." I gave one example to illustrate my point— "I remember an international mission conference I attended in Pattaya, Thailand. Every time I walked through the lobby, whether at breakfast or midnight, the ten stuffed chairs held hunched-over missionaries working on their laptops, taking advantage of the free wireless connection. I saw just as many men and women from southeast Asia, central America, and Africa in those chairs as from wealthier regions like Europe or North America. Christian workers may scrimp on clothing, entertainment, or other things … but not on Machines if they can help it!"

David heartily agreed and confessed that was precisely what scared him most. He was exceedingly cautious about divulging specific information, but he proceeded to relate several personal experiences of technology putting international Christian workers at grave risk:

- "Terrorists know how to manipulate captives, families, and mission agencies through technology. Instead of the traditional ransom note," Dose noted, "now captives can send messages in real time. Knowing that ransom emails or text messages were written just five minutes earlier really ratchets up the sense of urgency and pressure felt by people back home … despite the fact that the emails are always screened."

- "Cell phones send off locator signals that are picked up by cell phone towers every few minutes," Dose told me. "Terrorists or security officials can track missionaries' routes, speed of travel, and the location and duration of stops. They no longer need to interrogate missionaries for information, but instead they can simply track or bug the missionaries' cell phones and present them with a complete list of everywhere they have been for the past several weeks."

- "Laptops are often carelessly misplaced or stolen, whether in free or repressive countries. They may be stolen for money reasons," Dose cautioned, "but that doesn't mean they will not also be shared with security police who want to restrict Christian activity. One time a laptop was stolen from a missionary, apparently for financial reasons. Soon afterward, though, five missionary friends who were listed in his computer were called in for official government questioning."

- "BlackBerrys and smartphones are also very rich sources of all the information that terrorists or a hostile government would want about a Christian's networks and activities. There have been instances where police threatened ministry workers at gunpoint to retrieve and divulge information from one of those devices," Dose said. "I am now advising clients to arrange for a secret distress command that 'wipes' clean their server, so that sensitive information will not fall into the wrong hands."

David has a wonderful sense of humor, but he turns grave quickly because his business is deadly serious. "I remember a Western Christian who started a business in a Muslim country and had his laptop stolen," he recounted. "Unfortunately, the laptop contained materials about introducing Muslims to Christ. In most situations, that would lead to the Westerner's deportation and reprisals for any nationals who had dealt with him. In this case, the Westerner met with a far worse fate."

Machines can help provide relief to orphans and homeless in Burma, and they can also cause Christian workers to be deported, fired, or even killed. The Jekyll and Hyde nature of Machines is not exceptional but rather symptomatic of the global church's life at the Meeting of the Waters. Each of the Currents presents special opportunities for the global church, but each also presents perils that could well hamper God's work. My prayer is that the stories of Brian, Pete, and David will help the global church to navigate these murky issues with wisdom and discernment.

MACHINES
Representative Organizations

One of the most dramatic features of Machines is their myriad forms and uses, from providing disaster relief to conducting research to meeting basic physical needs to spreading the gospel. The global church is exceedingly creative and enterprising in its use of Machines to fulfill the Great Commission and the Great Commandment, and the following organizations represent a tiny sampling of the projects in which technology is central:

1. **Least of These International:** Least of These International (LOTI) produces research and innovative technologies to meet basic needs for communities in Haiti, Tanzania, and Kenya. LOTI educates indigenous leaders of nonprofits and churches to maintain and sustain the on-the-ground innovations and improvements. (www.lotint.org/about.html)

2. **Faith Comes By Hearing:** Faith Comes By Hearing (FCBH) records and distributes audio versions of the Bible in scores of languages to bring the church together and make disciples from every nation, tribe, language, and people. The Audio Bible, available on disc or MP3, offers God's Word in a format that connects with the world's 50-percent illiterate population. (www.faithcomesbyhearing.com)

3. **NOOMA:** NOOMA is a series of ten- to fourteen-minute films produced since 2002 by a nonprofit company called Flannel. From the outset, NOOMA was designed for "the millions of spiritually intrigued individuals that cannot relate to today's church or to traditional Christian media and content delivery." Each short story covers a specific topic, usually by portraying a modern-day parable and discussing it from a Christian perspective. The first

series features Rob Bell, teaching pastor at Mars Hill Bible Church in Grand Rapids, Michigan. Flannel distributes the films through its Web site. (www.nooma.com)

4. **Jesus Film:** The premiere Christian movie, *The Jesus Film,* was created by Bill Bright's Campus Crusade for Christ in 1976 to depict the life of Christ as accurately as possible, with primary dependence upon the gospel of Luke. The *New York Times* says that it is likely the most-watched motion picture of all time.[20] The Jesus Film Project's internal estimates show that the film has been viewed by almost 5.6 billion people (including repeat viewings) in nearly one hundred nations in over three hundred languages, and that over 225 million people made decisions for Christ after watching the film. The Jesus Film Project now works with thousands of missionaries around the world to show the film, sometimes in rudimentary, outdoor settings with audiences who have never seen a motion picture. (www.jesusfilm.org/film-and-media/watch-the-film)

5. **iTunes:** Hundreds of sermons and lessons are available as podcasts on iTunes and are developing huge word-of-mouth followings well beyond the pastors' home pulpits. Formerly these sermons were sold on audiocassettes through "tape ministries," but now iTunes offers listeners immediate access to sermons by pastors and teachers from around the world. For instance, *Christianity Today* wrote of Pastor Francis Chan, "His sermons consistently rank in the top 20 Christian podcasts on iTunes, in a group that includes Mark Driscoll and John Piper."[21]

6. **Jesus Central:** Incorporated in 2001, Jesus Central is a Web-based ministry that "helps people from all cultural and spiritual backgrounds learn about the person of Jesus." Jesus Central

offers historical and biographical information about Jesus, access to Bible verses and Jesus' quotations, theologians' writings on Jesus, and interactive classes and learning communities. The Jesus Central China Web site is entirely in Mandarin, which is the most common language for all Internet users under the age of thirty. (www.jesuscentral.com)

CHAPTER 7

Mediation

Civility in an Extreme World

The driver dropped me off for my late-night appointment with the famous Indonesian Muslim imam at our agreed meeting place, a closed restaurant some forty-five minutes from Jakarta's city center. My translator and I wound through the lounge and a closed banquet room, past stacked chairs and an empty buffet stand, and into a dark back room where we could make out three figures at a table at the far end. One of the men was the bodyguard, one was … well, I never did find out, and then there was Hasyim Muzadi.

I had been told I should meet Muzadi since he was the head of possibly the world's largest Muslim social and educational organization, the 47-million-strong Nahdlatul Ulama (NU).[1] I had some level of apprehension because I had never met with an international Muslim leader before, let alone one as prominent as Muzadi. He had been one of six Indonesian religious leaders invited to meet President Bush in Bali in 2003. In addition, of course, I was pretty spooked by the setting and details of the rendezvous.

Pak Muzadi ("Pak" is a title afforded to Indonesian elders and leaders) had a welcoming, if low-key demeanor. Indonesian culture is rich with an understated hospitality and mutual respect. Like many Indonesian officials and executives, he wore a colorful, shiny batik shirt with shirttails out and a kufi (Muslim prayer cap). As I spoke, he leaned in close and looked directly across the table into my eyes, often nodding in affirmation and agreement. I knew that, although he relied heavily on his translator, he understood much more English than he was letting on.

I was excited to be having this meeting, because I had come to believe that moderate Muslims like Pak Muzadi are central to peaceful international relations and to the global church's reconciliatory role. Increasingly, in all areas of society around the world, differences between groups are emphasized, suspicions and indignities are exaggerated, extreme actions are rewarded, and moderation far too often is disdained. Radical voices are inciting fragmentation at all corners of the globe and in all facets of society, and the voices of moderation caught in the middle are in difficult but critical positions. As it moves forward from the Meeting of the Waters, I believe that the global church must step into one of the world's greatest needs, the sixth Global Current—*Mediation.*

———

Theologian Martin Marty nailed the diagnosis of today's world: "[G]lobalization … introduces a vortex of bewildering economic and cultural change that can spark exclusivist or fundamentalist reactions."[2] One of the major causes in the rise of extremist groups around the world is an angry reaction to the homogenizing effect of Monoculture, which threatens to take away people's sense of identity and self-determinism. With battle lines drawn in an increasingly us-versus-them world, the global church and its leaders must step forward to meet a growing need for reconciliation and Mediation. The church's role as mediator will place it at the fault lines of the world's brewing crises:

- Political mediation is needed, as Web sites, blogs, and cable channels around the world feed polarization. In the United States, this is evident in permanent debates over gay marriage and abortion, but every country has similar conservative-liberal rifts. Both sides make impassioned, loud, and lengthy cases, but they rarely convince the other side of anything.

- Philosophical mediation will see Christians responding lovingly, as "new atheists" use varied media to belittle and bait religionists. A widely circulated Internet article alleged that only 1 or 2 percent of Americans claimed to be atheists in the 1950s, but that a recent poll shows 9 percent not believing in a creator and 12 percent being uncertain. Whatever the accuracy of those figures, the author of the article rightly concludes, "What is actually happening here and abroad is a great polarization."[3]

- Social mediation will be the only way that societies can ever deal with the increasing diversity of all types. Many people assume that intermixing will lead to greater tolerance, but that is not necessarily the case. Harvard sociologist Robert Putnam made waves in an important lecture on this point when he concluded, "The more we are brought into physical proximity with people of another race or ethnic background, the more we stick to 'our own' and the less we trust the 'other.'"[4]

- Ethnic mediation by the global church will help to defuse hatred and resentment among alienated ethnic, nationalist, and extremist groups all over the world. Fragmentation seems to be the norm in places as diverse as Tibet, Kosovo, Breslan, Baghdad and Tikrit, Rwanda, and Sudan. Alienated groups often harbor distorted conspiratorial views of what has gone wrong. They convince themselves that adopting extreme measures best addresses these affronts, real and imagined.[5]

- International mediation will be needed if Americans are to function in a world that has become widely anti-American. One journalist cites erosion of American power as "the core fact of recent years."[6] He wrote, "Global access to information now amounts to an immense a la carte menu. Networks escape control. To hundreds of millions of people accessing information for the first time, from central China to Kenya's Rift Valley, the United States can look exclusive and less relevant to their future."[7] Whereas, in previous eras, the United States could exert authority by virtue of its size and clout, that dynamic is diminishing.[8] More diverse opinions are available through the Internet, so readers can either purpose to obtain balanced perspectives or (perhaps more often the case) seek out those commentators who support their preexisting biases.

- Mission mediation will be necessary for Western followers of Christ facing global backlash to past colonialism, as our current efforts to evangelize are viewed by some as an effort to dominate.[9] Most fundamentally, the terms "Christian" and "missions" are great causes of division in some places. As a Thai believer explained, "[I]n the eyes of the Thai, to become a Christian means you can no longer be Thai. That's because in Thailand 'Christian' equals 'foreigner.'" He recounted an experience in which a Buddhist monk who was a friend of his had demonstrated great interest in his relationship with Jesus. The Buddhist monk was only interested, the Thai man realized, because he perceived that "Christianity and Jesus are two different things. Salvation is in Jesus, not in Christianity. If I had said I was a 'Christian,' the conversation would have ended at that point."[10]

- Class mediation will be a major role for the global church in the face of growing disparities between different strata of society—well-educated and under-educated, white collar and blue collar. Many people thought that education and communication would erase those gaps, but *New York Times* journalist David Brooks claims the opposite is happening:

> [Many have assumed that] as people become better educated, primitive passions like tribalism and nationalism would fade away [and as] communications technology improved, there would be greater cooperation and understanding. [But in fact], religion hasn't withered; it has become stronger and more fundamentalist. Nationalism and tribalism haven't faded away.... Communications technology hasn't brought people closer together; it has led to greater cultural segmentation, across the world.... [As] people are empowered by greater wealth and education, cultural differences become more pronounced, not less, as different groups chase different visions of the good life, and react in aggressive ways to perceived slights to their cultural dignity.[11]

- Economic mediation is a pressing need as financial crises occur and globalization produces enormous wealth for many, exaggerating financial disparities between rich and poor. In a farewell address at a global conference, Nelson Mandela, the former president of South Africa, wondered, "Is globalism only going to benefit the powerful? Does it offer nothing to men, women, and children ravaged by the violence of poverty?"[12] Elias Zerhouni, the head of the National Institutes for Health, had a similar experience during a trip to Africa and Asia a few years ago. It was then that he learned that malaria was once again a big problem, after near elimination in the 1970s. He concluded that there are "two divergent globalizations going on at the same time on our planet. One globalization is that of an increasingly connected world, as aptly described by Thomas Friedman. But the other globalization is that of an increasingly disconnected world where knowledge may actually be decreasing and where poverty and disease are on a steady climb."[13]

• Religious mediation must become a natural, constant pursuit of the global church. It will be required amid militant Hindutva in India,[14] Buddhist nationalism in Sri Lanka, Orthodox Church repression of competitors in Russia, and Christian violence in Nigeria.[15] And then there is Islam. Harvard scholar Samuel Huntington wrote an influential article predicting an inevitable "clash of civilizations" between Christianity and Islam, noting that Islam has "bloody borders" wherever it exists.[16] Feelings between Christians and Muslims range from Huntington's pessimism to sadness, defiance, sympathy, or desire for revenge.

Jakarta, Indonesia is about as far from the United States as a person can get. Like most Americans, I was somewhat familiar with other southeast Asian countries like Australia, Vietnam, and the Philippines, but not at all with Indonesia. If that were not enough, I was feeling even more disoriented as I stared at the impassive features of Pak Muzadi. I knew of his unsuccessful 2004 bid for president of Indonesia, when he shared the ticket with former president Megawati Setiawati Sukarnoputri, and he won 26 percent of the vote. One political pundit had called the even-tempered moderate candidate "boring," but as I sat across from him he seemed pretty intense.

Some might say I was out of my depth, and I think he knew that … so he kindly schooled me.

He explained, through his translator, how Indonesia's constitution aligned the country neatly with democratic Western nations like the United States. In the Indonesian constitution, the central principle of *Pancasila* emphasizes monotheism and a harmonious, communal society where religious groups coexist. Five religions enjoy official preferred status in Indonesia—Islam, Buddhism, Hinduism, Protestant Christianity, and Catholic Christianity. Indonesia has a history of moderate Islam, Muzadi emphasized, and he was intent on using that platform to help spread moderation, tolerance, democracy, and human rights throughout southeast Asia.

The translator's accent was thick, but I was desperate to catch Pak's drift, because I had lots to learn; this was not the kind of Muslim leader I had seen portrayed in the media.

I asked him about the efforts of militant Muslims to impose sharia law, the harsh and oppressive system of Islamic rules, in Indonesia. I knew that was one of the main themes in his leadership of NU, and he had a lot to say about it, as he insisted that sharia law is a very bad fit for Indonesian society. He said that militant Muslims needed to remember that they live in moderate Indonesia.

Muzadi pressed his agenda further, then, emphasizing that the United States, Britain, and other Western countries should support moderate Muslim groups that resist radicalization. The logic and moral merit of the idea made immediate sense to me, even as I was keenly aware of the political complications, risks, and barriers.

Indonesia is a linchpin country in global affairs, and therefore in the global church today. It is the world's fourth-largest country, with over 230 million citizens, and the largest Muslim country with up to 200 million adherents.[17] Fully 40 percent of the entire world's trade flows through the Straits of Malacca, just ten miles from Indonesia's northeast shore.[18] The straits are an important passageway between China and India—and also between Europe, the Suez Canal, the oil-exporting countries of the Persian Gulf, and the busy ports of Singapore, Hong Kong, Taiwan, and Tokyo. Because of its prominence in the Muslim world and its key trade location, Indonesia is a battleground country of supreme strategic interest.

As I learned from Pak Muzadi, the current environment in Indonesia is in frightening flux as it sits squarely in the crosshairs of militant Islam. Catholic Archbishop Henri Tessier's observation about Algeria applies equally well to Indonesia: "The central tension ... is not between Muslims and Christians, but between Muslims and other Muslims, as competing currents within ... society struggle for domination."[19] In Indonesia, as in other countries around the world, moderate Muslims bear the brunt of hostility, pressure, and persecution from militant Muslims.

A Pew Foundation study put a fine point on it:

> Today a virtual civil war is occurring within Islam—a struggle for the soul of the faith between militant Islamists ... and moderates who in varying ways seek to reclaim the best of their heritage and join the mainstream of economic and political life on the global stage.... [M]ilitants ... have been successful to varying degrees in "intimidating, marginalizing, or silencing moderate Muslims."[20]

Influential Muslims from outside of Indonesia seek to encourage Indonesian moderates to switch to the more militant Saudi-style Islam. A Rand Corporation study notes that, though radical Muslims are a small minority in almost all Muslim nations, they nevertheless have influence disproportionate to their numbers.[21]

In Indonesia, the number of militant Muslims is estimated at much less than one million people—less than one percent of all Muslims in that country—but they are well-funded and well-organized. Their stated aim is the complete elimination of Christianity in the country. Indonesian businessmen, ministry leaders, pastors, and a dozen Parliament members told me that their country is a breeding ground for radical Islam for several reasons:

- Most obviously, the large concentration of Muslims;

- Widespread dire poverty that breeds desperation and frustration;

- Very low levels of education; and

- Geographic proximity to the Middle East and easy access to the rest of the world.

The primary tools that radical Muslims use to recruit moderates are the lure of vast Saudi oil wealth and the fear of violence. Money and power. For example, in October 2002, Islamic terrorists carried out a suicide bombing in a Bali nightclub, which took 202 lives. The involvement of outside extremists in Indonesia typifies modern terrorism and proves the political adage "the bombs of Belfast were born in Boston." In this case, though, the bombs were probably born in Riyadh.

As I thought about my own circles of friends and professional peers, I suspected that many of them would view my meeting with Muzadi as a fool's errand. Not surprisingly, that sentiment runs both ways; in an interview Muzadi noted, "The vast Muslim majority that feels nothing but revulsion for terror is often suspicious of the West."[22] Without voices of Mediation, that situation can be all too common in today's world—parties in intractable positions eyeing each other from across party lines, national borders, theologies, ideologies, lifestyles, or races. I left the meeting grateful that I had at least closed some of the distance, and was able to eye Pak Muzadi across the table on friendly terms instead of across oceans.

I have no illusions that my meeting with Pak Muzadi made any progress toward reducing barriers between the United States and Indonesia or between Christians and Muslims. I do know, though, that the meeting began to bridge the divide in my own heart. As I recommitted to my own role in being a mediator in an age of polarization, I recalled Aleksandr Solzhenitsyn's words in *Gulag Archipelago:* "It was only when I lay there on rotting prison straw that I sensed within myself the first stirrings of good. Gradually it was disclosed to me that the line separating good and evil passes not through states, not between classes, nor between political parties either—but right through every human heart—and through all human hearts."[23]

Against the larger backdrop of religious beliefs, cultural issues like dress take on added significance. During a time when I was perturbed by the immodest fashions that my own teenage daughters gravitated toward, Omar, an acquaintance in Jordan, told me of his family's predicament in the face of fundamentalist Islamic inroads. Since the Iranian revolution in 1979, he had seen a marked increase in Jordan and other Arab nations in women wearing Muslim head coverings. This concerned him greatly, because he viewed it as a sure sign of the spread of militant Islam in Jordan. He associated the traditional and restrictive clothing with repression of women's rights, and he feared that other violations of rights were sure to follow, for both women and men.

Omar's consternation grew as more and more of his teenage daughter's friends began covering up. Famous in the Arab world for being a moderate, progressive society with religious freedom, Jordan—like Indonesia—faces pressure from fundamentalist sources to embrace a more strident, militant form of Islam. His fear was not, Omar explained, whether his daughter could wear the miniskirts she loved. Omar feared that his country's beloved peace was at risk.[24]

His fears were well founded. The militant Islamists made their next move a few weeks after our conversation: Bombs tore through the lobby of Amman's Grand Hyatt Hotel, slammed a wedding party at the Radisson SAS Hotel down the street, and exploded at the Days Inn Hotel, all within minutes of each other. Fifty-nine people died, and about one hundred were wounded. Jordan, with its peace treaty and historic ties with both Washington and neighboring Israel, had become a nettlesome inconvenience to extremists.

Several days after the bombings, thousands of Jordanians marched in the streets in protest, expressing defiance and outrage. "Not in Jordan!" their signs and chants said. By marching in protest, Jordanians were sending a signal that their land would not be a site for sectarian or religious conflict—or for terrorism. When I read the account, I recalled Omar's indignation. He had forewarned, "This is how wars start. It starts with fabric and fashions, and then it becomes bombs and death."

Moderate Muslims in places like Jordan and Indonesia are in an awful pinch. If they cannot practice moderation in peace, then what alternatives might they choose—and might their children choose? Certainly, the siren song of violence will continue to beckon them.

Pak Muzadi taught me, "There are two possible effective responses to radical Islam: to seek to eradicate violence and terrorism, and to strengthen moderate Islam." The United States government has historically proceeded gingerly and sporadically in engaging with moderate Muslims, but it is significant that Secretary of State Hillary Clinton's first international trip was to Indonesia. While there, she praised the Indonesian government for its fight against Islamic extremism. The government is adapting, and the church should too.

I believe that, in the coming years, the Christian church should be first in line to practice Mediation (without ever compromising truth, of course). Practicing reconciliation with people of different religions, ethnicities, customs, or beliefs is a practice every follower of Christ can pursue, and not just "professionals" like pastors, scholars, foundation directors, or missionaries. A foreign mission scholar wrote that "pluralism is not a philosophy reserved for the classroom; it's the worldview of the common person.... In the face of global pluralism, the church must proclaim Jesus Christ with theological integrity, critical contextualization, and above all, with an open and transparent spirit."[25]

Dr. Richard Mouw, president of Fuller Theological Seminary, wrote a book called *Uncommon Decency,* articulating the charge for all followers of Christ to be reconcilers. One takeaway notion powerfully illuminated my understanding of polarization of all kinds, including within my own church denomination. "[One] of the real problems in modern life," Mouw wrote, citing Martin Marty, "is that the people who are good at being civil often lack strong convictions and people who have strong convictions often lack civility."[26] I have often placed more value on being correct and accurate than on being connected and accepting of people—even when I cannot condone their positions or behavior. Mouw elaborated: "We need to find a way of combining a civil outlook with a 'passionate intensity' about our convictions. The real challenge is to come up with a *convicted civility.*"[27]

That kind of approach should be normal behavior within the global church as we emulate Jesus Christ. Other institutions have often failed here. Governments ill-advisedly ignore citizens' longings for transcendent meaning in life. Militaries often fail to understand the role that religion plays in conflicts. American schools are supposed to allow freedom of religion, but public school teachers fear that God-talk will endanger their jobs, and college professors sometimes believe that faith equates with ignorance or intolerance. Followers of Christ must step into the void between factions—sometimes as prophets, expecting condemnation, but more often as peacemakers, encouragers, and friends.

In today's world, the absence of peaceful discussion about religious differences often seems to lead to suspicion and hostility. The void affects Christians and people of other faiths equally, as so few people seem to know how to talk inoffensively about their faith with others who feel differently. Dr. Eboo Patel recounted his disillusionment as a Muslim doctoral student during his Rhodes Scholar days at Oxford University: "In all the sociology courses on identity ... the issue of religion rarely came up.... The one three-letter word that I rarely heard during my time in college: God. [We] took diversity seriously, but it was always about blacks and whites, poor folks and rich folks, urbanites and suburbanites; never about Muslims, Christians, and Jews."[28]

While multifaith dialogue will never guarantee peace, it is certainly a good start. In his book, *Acts of Faith,* Patel wrote,

> W. E. B. DuBois famously said, "The problem of the twentieth century is the problem of the color line." I believe that the twenty-first century will be shaped by the question of the faith line....[29] As a devout Muslim, I certainly want to preserve the uniqueness of my religion. But you can go too far in that direction, ... which is the thinking that religious differences are so great that we can't even talk....[30] The truth is, our religious traditions have competing theological claims, and we simply have to accept those....[31] [One time, I hired] an Evangelical Christian ... [and] she firmly believed that Christianity was a uniquely true religion and that Jesus was Lord and Savior. By proclaiming our strong

commitments to our respective faiths, even
intimating that we believed that what we each
had was superior; neither of us was offended by
the other's faith commitment. To the contrary,
it had created a common bond.[32]

The fear among Christians, especially conservative ones, is that interfaith dialogues will require them to compromise important beliefs. But Dr.
Mouw addresses that point concisely:

> Christian civility does not commit us to a
> *relativistic* perspective. Being civil does not
> mean we cannot criticize what goes on around
> us.... In the final analysis, the choice between
> religious perspectives has to do with mutu-
> ally exclusive truth claims about reality and
> goodness. No amount of dialogue will make
> those differences go away. I cannot accept
> a call to interreligious dialogue that rejects
> Christianity's claims to uniqueness. And,
> frankly, I know Jews and Muslims who would
> also reject that approach.[33]

Mouw helped me to realize that I have long focused, first and naturally, on conviction, which I base upon firm theological principles. Lately,
though, I have increasingly had civility on my heart, probably because of
my global exposure. Never a fan of interfaith dialogue in the past, I now
view it as a corrective to my soul, an act of love to strangers in my midst,
and a winsome witness to the world.

So, when I was asked in 2004 to join a dialogue with Muslim leaders in Richmond, Virginia, I considered it with a combination of excitement and nerves. Local Muslims began the dialogue because they feared that, in the post-9/11 environment, they were susceptible to stereotyping and discrimination. They had read that evangelical Christians were politically powerful and visible and appeared to take faith matters seriously, so they sought to start a dialogue with leaders from that community; they wanted to be understood as well as to become more civically engaged. I agreed to participate.

The group that convened the dialogue was a local interfaith organization called Hope for the Cities. Not surprisingly, they had very few evangelical contacts. The dialogue's initial evangelical cohort ended up being quite a diverse mix, including some who did not agree with any tenets of evangelicalism. But that was part of the learning process for me too.

By the way, I am fully aware that these are very uncomfortable ideas for many. An Egyptian pastor friend believes I am naively appeasing Muslims. My mother has never objected, but I think she may have her doubts. My friends, who frequently find me eccentric, don't really ask me about it. And my children just smile and shake their heads as they hear their father talking about his new friends Muhammad, Issad, Harum, Miriam, and Youssef.

At our first meeting, the Christians and Muslims were sent to different rooms, given a discussion question, and asked to reassemble in thirty minutes to report to the group. The question was, "What are some actions for which your group would like to apologize to the other group?" As we Christians assembled, the first answer was easy: We would apologize for the Crusades, which was obviously a cop-out since none of us had been present or bore any blame.

Then some of the liberals-in-evangelical-clothing suggested that we apologize for evangelizing. Biding my time, I eventually spoke up, "I just want you to know that I won't join in that apology. You see, the New Testament contains the Great Commission, and it's a biblical mandate telling us to do just that—to evangelize. I will," I continued, "apologize for Christians evangelizing coercively or insensitively, but not for the mere act of evangelization."

I had no idea whether my stance would scuttle the dialogue before it started; not being an experienced dialoguer, I did not know if my objection was egregiously out of bounds. I felt, though, that if something as basic as the Great Commission endangered the dialogue, then these Muslims did not *really* want to be interacting with real, live evangelicals.

My objection made its way back to the entire group, and I braced for waves of Muslim wrath. But Muhammad piped up, "Of course you should not apologize for evangelizing!" and Harum said, "We evangelize too—it's a free country."

That and future exchanges taught me many lessons. I learned that humility, humor, and candor go a long way—and are acceptable temporary substitutes for expertise and sophistication. I also learned that, as people of strict laws and requirements themselves, moderate Muslims appreciate resolve and discipline in Christians. I have found that many Muslims hold little respect for people who take their faith lightly, and some Muslims assume (and sometimes rightly) that American Christians are permissive and morally lax.

I have also realized that the bar is set low for evangelical Christians in interfaith dialogue; the Muslims were simply relieved, I think, that I was not wearing a sandwich board and ranting.

After several monthly group meetings, I privately began to meet Muhammad at Starbucks. He had immigrated to the United States from Pakistan as a teenager, and now worked as an engineer nearing retirement at a huge manufacturer. We talked a lot about Islam, and I felt very free to ask his take on world events. We talked about his job—at the time a secret project requiring long commutes. Just as often, he wanted to gripe about Sooner football, which he had lived and died for since his college days at the University of Oklahoma.

I also had lunch with Harum several times; a pharmacologist from Lebanon, he had studied at the Sorbonne in Paris. English—which he speaks impeccably—is his third language. A very smart guy, he remains prominent in local civic life because of his desire and skill at networking and dialoguing. We often run into each other now at events around town, and our friendship means a lot to me.

My wife and I invited Issad and Miriam and their two children over to dinner, and we had a delightful evening. Issad is from Iran, and Miriam is from Pakistan and Saudi Arabia. They are in their early thirties and do not stand out at all, except for Miriam's head scarf. We talked about how to teach conservative values (and we share many of them) to our children. I misstepped one time when I offered a marshmallow to their daughter, not realizing that it had pork in it and was therefore *haraam* (forbidden). When we later hosted a graduation party for another friend, Youssef, we were more careful about our food choices.

After several monthly dialogue sessions, I had developed a real affinity for Muslims in my midst. I also cared more about Richmond being a welcoming home for them. I had heard Miriam speak about the stares cast her way because of her *hijab* whenever she went out in public spaces. Knowing how highly Arab immigrants value hospitality, I was sad to think of fellow Richmonders and Americans feeling like intruders or enemies in their own town.

My knowledge about the radical-moderate Muslim strife in Indonesia and around the world pressed home the importance of affirming the Muhammads, Harums, Issads and Miriams, and Youssefs in Richmond. For me, meeting with Muslims is the Christian thing to do.

In the introductory lecture of her popular Harvard University course on world religions, renowned professor Diana Eck always told her students, "If you only know one religion, you don't know any."[34] I believe that statement has some truth in it, because my exposure to Islam has clearly made me a better mediator for Jesus Christ. I have more compassion for those who are different; more humility about things I do and do not know; more resolve in stating the things I do believe; less concern about whether others think I am "right"; less fear in talking to others who are very different from me; and more ability to relate to others without an agenda.

In the future, the world needs for the global church to learn to love and work with others, be they Muslims, Hindus, Buddhists, animists, or atheists. Is there danger or personal risk in personal outreach to people or groups that express hostility toward us? Only God knows, just as only He foreknew all of the risks that His Son would incur among people like me.

Our efforts at reconciliation can start today—in our towns, cities, school boards, youth soccer leagues, schools, workplaces, PTAs, Girl Scouts troops, and neighborhood associations. If Muslim immigrants never experience love and warmth from Christians, then our witness is weakened. Ever since my trip to Indonesia and my involvement with the interfaith dialogue, I have strived to be an accepting, curious, and friendly follower of Christ toward Muslims I meet in Richmond. Those are admittedly baby steps compared to the huge volume of grave issues the world faces, but they are tiny doses of Mediation that I am able to administer in my part of a polarizing world.

MEDIATION
Representative Organizations

Mediation requires great restraint in dealing with people of very different perspectives. All of the organizations mentioned below work to promote peace and reconciliation where there is conflict, particularly in the area of religion. These organizations are very scattered in their theological and political perspectives, though, and evangelical Christian perspectives seem to be underrepresented. There is an acute need, therefore, for Christians to venture into the world of Mediation, wielding our faith humbly, respectfully, and confidently.

1. **Institute for Global Engagement:** Since 2000, the Washington DC-based Institute for Global Engagement (IGE) has employed the concept of "relational diplomacy" to equip local governments worldwide to promote religious freedom. IGE currently operates in many countries throughout Asia, Africa, and the Middle East. IGE was founded by Ambassador Robert Seiple, the former president of World Vision and the U.S. State Department's first Ambassador-at-Large for International Religious Freedom. (www.globalengage.org)

2. **International Center for Religion and Diplomacy:** The International Center for Religion and Diplomacy uses religion as a means for conflict resolution, to prevent and resolve conflicts in various parts of the world. Central to the Center's approach is its ability to capitalize on the positive role that religious leaders and institutions can play in building trust and overcoming differences. Founder Douglas Johnston is editor of *Religion, The Missing Dimension of Statecraft*.[35] (www.icrd.org)

3. **EastWest Institute:** Founded in 1980, the EastWest Institute (EWI) is an independent, nonpartisan, action-oriented international organization addressing dangerous fault lines that threaten peace and security. EWI convenes leaders from government, business, military, media, and other sectors, from the developing and developed worlds, to "prevent conflict and manage challenges posed by rapid global change."[36] EWI has offices in New York, Brussels, and Moscow. Os Guinness, a well-known evangelical Christian author and speaker, is a senior fellow at EWI. (www.ewi.info)

4. **First Freedom Center:** First Freedom Center was founded in 1984 to increase understanding and respect for religious freedom in diverse communities worldwide, through education about freedom of thought, conscience, and belief. It is nonpolitical and nondenominational, simply emphasizing that all persons are entitled to freedom of religion unfettered by the State. The Center's programs include national essay contests for high school students, resources for teachers to use in their classrooms, and exhibits on religious freedom. (www.firstfreedom.org)

5. **The Becket Fund:** The Becket Fund is a public-interest law firm and educational group that defends religious freedom in the court of law, the court of public opinion, and the academy. The Becket Fund believes that the religious impulse is natural to human beings, so its lawyers provide legal support to people of all faiths, publicizing those cases through major media outlets, and generating scholarship about them. Becket's expertise, combined with the religious diversity of its clients, has earned it credibility before conservative and liberal judges, mainstream media, and legal

scholars. Each December, Becket issues its "Ebenezer Award" to an individual or group responsible for "the most ridiculous affront to the Christmas and Hanukkah holidays."[37] (www.becketfund.org)

CHAPTER 8

Memory

The Lingering Past

It was obviously a corpse, but I tried not to stare as the woman peddled past me with the long, stiff, wrapped-up bundle balanced across her bike's back fender. Visiting Uganda, a country where more than 1.5 million people have died from AIDS[1] and most people do not have cars, I reminded myself that I should not be surprised to see someone bicycling a loved one to the cemetery.

Even at midnight, the roads in Uganda's villages and cities are teeming. Street vendors hustle fish, live chickens, music, vegetables, auto parts, magazines, appliances, beer, clothing, furniture, and everything else a Ugandan might want. A steady stream of foot traffic wanders along the road—mothers with children in tow, boys with bunches of fresh bananas or firewood on their backs, women carrying water jugs on their heads, men riding bicycles with building supplies strapped on every which way, farmers herding cows and goats, throngs at taxi stands, and groups of friends sharing stories.

Uganda is, in many ways, a typical east African country, but it also has significant distinctives. Most notably, it is a country that is especially plagued by its "back story"—a term that literary critics use to describe relevant historical events that lie behind the current state of affairs. During long car rides, late-night talks, break times at conferences, and wonderful protracted meals, one Ugandan after another described their country as a place continually haunted by ghosts of the past. Whether in Uganda or other countries, when historical events or circumstances hold powerful sway in modern life, it is a reflection of the power of the seventh Global Current—*Memory.*

Life in the twenty-first century is saturated with experiences that are new and unprecedented, experiences that roll out at a pace that allows for little reflection or retrospection. I am reminded of cars in Delhi, India, where both rearview mirrors are folded in (and are therefore unusable). My friend there justified it to me: "It's hard enough to drive in this place, just concentrating on what's going on in front of me. Why do I care what's happening back there?"

That attitude resonates with many Americans—Memory being an especially difficult Current for Americans to grasp. We are slow to appreciate the importance of the past, partly because our own history is so short. This struck home with me several years ago when my family hosted Benni, a German exchange student. We drove an hour with Benni to Williamsburg, the town that was Virginia's capital during colonial times. Benni laughed to see thousands of tourists from around America visiting this restored village from the eighteenth century ... an era that his countrymen regard as modern history.

Americans are generally characterized by short-term orientation, in that they believe that they owe little to history. Their past does not define their future. Americans' unique self-image is suffused with ideals like the American Dream, the rags-to-riches success story, and the belief that "the sky's the limit."

Memory is indeed relatively foreign to Americans and easy to overlook, but it is nonetheless powerful and pervasive. For instance, America's attitude toward Memory often shapes her foreign relations. I once heard a foreign relations expert note, "When Americans say 'That's history,' they mean 'It's over.' When other people around the world say 'That's history,' they mean 'Draw up the swords.'"[2] There is a great risk here: That Memory blind spot can cripple American foreign policy, and also America's churches, as they seek to serve the global church in the years to come. Even in a future that wows us with its earthshaking change, the past will nevertheless be a powerful player. After all, there is never a fresh start-date, a time when the successes and failures of the past cease to matter. In spiritual matters, likewise, generational and historical legacies loom large.

In Uganda, Memory is deadly serious. Uganda deals with two streams of Memory—first, the lingering effects of more than half a century of British rule, and second, the trauma from twenty years of brutal dictatorships. This complex history of domination and repression, both at the hands of colonial powers and homegrown despots, has created a nation where today is often a servant to yesterday. Memory is in play all around the world, and nowhere more than in Uganda.[3]

Postcolonialism is the world's most common form of Memory. All told, Uganda was under British rule for eighty-five years. Uganda's colonial period arguably began when missionaries arrived from London in 1877 and then continued when Great Britain claimed it as a protectorate in 1894 during Europe's "scramble for Africa."

In the middle of the twentieth century, the world saw a steady progression of countries breaking free from colonial rule, with Uganda (in 1962) and thirty-three other countries gaining independence between 1956 and 1966.[4] After so many years of political, military, and social subjugation, "postcolonial" people emerged into independence with untold scars and baggage. The ingrained cultural norms that persist after colonial rule can include servility, complacency, distrust, resentment, and most of all, dependency. Ugandans I spoke with used all of those words to describe their countrymen and their country's acute case of postcolonialism.

Tragically, Uganda also suffers from an additional version of Memory—the aftereffects of decades under murderous tyrant-leaders. After emerging from colonial rule in 1962, Uganda immediately went on to be terrorized by two tyrants, Milton Obote and Idi Amin. Under their rule, as many as one million Ugandans died at the hands of the government or insurgencies. The chain of dictators ended in 1985, but Memory extends their influence for generations. This is hardly surprising, for most adults in Uganda today recall childhoods and student years filled with fear, suspicion, and loss. One forty-year-old friend told me he never wore his watch on the streets as a child or university student, since he knew that Amin's soldiers would relieve him of it. History like that does not just disappear, but instead Memory colors the way affected victims live their lives with children and grandchildren. Memory, by definition, lingers.

It was when I heard the tale about Pastor Isaac Wagaba that I developed a deep appreciation for the unique place of Memory in places like Uganda. Isaac was a young pastor during the reign of Idi Amin in the early 1970s. Amin was the infamous world-renowned tyrant who dubbed himself "His Excellency President for Life, Field Marshal Al Hadji Doctor Idi Amin, VC, DSO, MC, Lord of All the Beasts of the Earth and Fishes of the Sea, and Conqueror of the British Empire in Africa in General and Uganda in Particular."[5] Amin viciously persecuted Christians, and his thugs rounded up pastors of the (necessarily) underground church and threw them into the Nile Mansion, a government-seized hotel that had been converted into a prison and torture chamber.

One morning, soldiers showed up at Isaac and Rebecca's house. They had been harassing Isaac for a while by interrogating him, his family, and his friends. This time, though, they looted and burned the house, shoved Isaac into a truck, and drove him away. Rebecca and her children were able to escape into the jungle, since it was Isaac whom the soldiers wanted.

After several days of deprivation at the Nile Mansion, a blindfolded Isaac had a decision to make. He and the other hungry, frightened pastors could convert to Islam and be circumcised, whereupon they would be set free … or they would be murdered. Several of the pastors renounced their faith and were led away. The rest of the captives, including Isaac, refused to deny Jesus as Christ and were shot. After the bullets ripped through Isaac, he collapsed in a heap and his body was pitched onto a truck with the other pastors. In a ritual that was commonplace in 1970's Uganda, the bodies were carted away and dumped into massive graves.

My daughter Rachel and I traveled to Buziika, Uganda on a beautiful summer day to visit the house where Isaac was seized. At the compound's metal gate, we were met with typical Ugandan greetings: those light-up-the-room smiles, loud laughter, two-cheek kisses, and multiple-clasp, lingering handshakes. Rebecca had prepared a massive lunch for us—chapati bread, green banana mash, rice, chicken, and greens. Ugandans are rarely in a hurry, and as our long lunch drifted easily into post-lunch conversation, my guests led me to the chair of honor. A bad combination there—jostling van travel, jet lag, a heavy lunch, and an overstuffed chair. I was kept awake, though, by one of the most riveting stories I have ever heard.

Isaac told Rachel and me the rest of his story with a twinkle of wonderment in his eyes. I knew he had recited his story thousands of times, but he clearly relished it anew with each telling.

He recalled being dumped into a massive open grave along with the other bodies. Near death, bleeding heavily from gunshot wounds to his arm and leg, he somehow crawled out of the mound of corpses. The last thing he remembers is a voice that told him, "Isaac, I will make you a father of the fatherless." He passed out on the side of the road.

His next conscious memory is of waking in the home of herdsmen who had rescued him. Those "good Samaritans" took him to a local hospital for treatment, where the doctors cared for him in secret. Amin's army had learned of a surviving pastor and combed the countryside in search of the one that got away. Isaac eventually managed to escape to Kenya, and after five years of correspondence, reunited in Uganda with Rebecca. Together they purposed to live out his newfound calling and began Canaan Children's Home. Today, Canaan Children's Home shelters dozens of orphans from AIDS and war, redeeming Isaac's horrific execution.

Nevertheless, Uganda is a country grounded in strife and war for the Wagabas and their generation, now in their mid-fifties. Under Amin, regular citizens lived in constant fear of robbery or assault by roving bands of renegade army soldiers, and Christians routinely suffered persecution for their faith. Today, many Ugandan orphans are refugees from yet another unspeakably grisly twenty-year war in northern Uganda.

Memory of this sort cannot be evaded. Any psychologist will tell you that Memory must eventually be faced. Ugandan citizens, and indeed the very culture, are extremely resilient, but they bear the scars of an unspeakable past.

Thirty years after Isaac's arrest, I sat in the rebuilt house that Amin's soldiers had once torched. While Isaac showed me the scar where a bullet had ripped through his left shoulder, he talked about the restoration and redemption God had made possible.

Like all of the Currents, Memory has both positive and negative effects. In Uganda, Memory persists and hobbles many, today and for years to come. On the other hand, in a classic parable of Christian redemption, Isaac Wagaba's "death" birthed him into a new role as father to the fatherless at Canaan Children's Home. Christians and the global church, it seems, have the ultimate remedy for a bad case of Memory.

Damoni Kitabire was born several hours outside of Kampala, Uganda, to a subsistence farmer and his wife in a very poor rural village. Even as an adult, he often made the long drive from his lovely Kampala house back to his home village to attend weddings, birthdays, and other family events.

He visited the village more often when his three daughters were young and still thought the trips were fun. The lure for his daughters to visit relatives in the rural village (without indoor plumbing) decreased, though, as they grew into big-city teenagers. As the father of three children, I could relate.

Educated Ugandans, in their British vernacular, say Damoni always was "clever." He attended a flagship university of east Africa, Makerere University in Kampala. He was bright enough to win a scholarship that enabled him to earn a master's degree in finance in Glasgow, Scotland. After returning to Kampala he responded to an advertisement in *The Economist* magazine and was hired to work for the International Monetary Fund in Washington DC for four years. During that time his wife, a doctor whom he had met during university, earned her master's in public health at Johns Hopkins University in Baltimore, Maryland. Eventually, Damoni, Florence, and their three girls returned to Kampala, where he was named Macro-Advisor for the Ministry of Finance, Planning, and Economic Development of the Republic of Uganda.

While sharing a meal with me one night in my hotel room, Damoni and I talked about the impact of Memory in Uganda. As one of the highest-ranking finance officials in Uganda, and now a lead economist with the African Development Bank, he approached Memory from an economic perspective.

He asked me if I had noticed anything unusual about traffic lights and credit cards in Uganda. When I stared at him blankly, he laughed at me and admitted that it was a trick question: Both were either nonexistent or nonfunctioning. That, he said, summed up Uganda's woeful economy. In Kampala, Uganda's capital city of 1.5 million people, there were two traffic lights at the time—one of which worked. There were very few road signs, fewer traffic lines, and countless potholes. Uganda's abysmal road and traffic conditions were clearly substantial deterrents to foreign investment in the country.

Credit cards were seldom used because Uganda had a simple cash economy. One night I attempted to take Damoni and his family to downtown

Kampala for dinner at a nice restaurant, which claimed to accept credit cards. I attempted to pay for the meal with several different cards but, after extensive confusion and questioning, I finally paid in cash. After that, I stocked up on Ugandan shillings for future meals.

As we chatted, Damoni explained to me that foreign investment in Uganda was minimal. I was shocked to learn that, at the time of my visit, fully 40 percent of Uganda's budget was "donor-funded"—aid simply donated by other nations or non-government agencies. I had not known that Uganda was practically a charity, a nonprofit nation. For instance, Damoni told me that the World Bank was giving Uganda about 200 million dollars annually and the United Kingdom was giving over 50 million dollars. While the revenue was much-needed, Damoni noted that it was not guaranteed into the future and was subject to arbitrary or sudden reduction or even cessation. That left Uganda both dependent and uncertain.[6] The tragic problem with such heavy reliance on donor-funded revenue, Damoni pointed out, was that it allowed Uganda to put off paying its own way.

Even I could piece that together. These men and women had grown up in an era when the predatory army made travel unsafe and all ventures subject to arbitrary confiscation or termination. Their parents had grown up in a colonial environment where most Ugandans' ambitions were minimized or rechanneled. And the country's money came not from private initiative but from overseas charity. It all caused, Damoni said, a pervasive passivity among Ugandans, of whom so little had been expected for so long. More than a few Ugandans I met noted that Ugandans had only been taught to take and not to earn or give. That is postcolonialism.

The lack of foreign investment, Damoni said, could also be seen in the absence of fast-food chains. While KFC, Starbucks, Burger King, and McDonald's dot urban landscapes in much of the developing world—including former communist countries that have only allowed private enterprise for ten or fifteen years—the only foreign interests that people could point to in Kampala at that time were a South African grocery store chain and a Pepsi-Cola plant. Damoni explained that fast-food companies did not invest in Uganda because there was not enough of an around-the-clock market for fast food, whether because of poverty or lack of mobility or consumption habits. Further, he noted that Uganda does not have a large-enough educated workforce to staff foreign franchises.

All of these symptoms, Damoni noted, sprung largely from the effect of Memory. Put simply, Uganda was stuck in the past. For a long time, a huge portion of Uganda's economic support was given and controlled by other countries. Those are characteristics of postcolonialism, and they indicate that Uganda will be dependent well into the future.

One of the more interesting findings in the Listening Tour was the Latin American country whose residents consistently referred to their country's inferiority complex. The phrases they used were unambiguous:

- "used to losing in things";

- "expect to play the supporting role";

- "for centuries, a culture of silence and timidity";

- "everything that is foreign is good, and what's our own is bad."

A Guatemalan friend noted his own country's postcolonial complex and pointed out how it affects the Guatemalan church. More than a century ago, he said, missionaries to his country never emphasized financial stewardship because they assumed the Guatemalans would always be poor. They assumed ongoing dependency for Guatemala and, no surprise, stewardship and generosity remain low in the Guatemalan church today. The same phenomenon occurred with Guatemalan attitudes toward international missions. The early missionaries assumed that they were already at the ends of the earth and that Guatemalans would always follow and never lead, so they did not attempt to inculcate a heart for missions. These Memory issues point to a need today for the global church to emphasize training and to strengthen leaders among indigenous Guatemalans. If possible, ministries in Guatemala should not be led by people from other countries.

Regarding Uganda, Damoni acknowledged that Memory contributed to current low aspirations and low confidence. He also noted, though, that people with low ambitions and accomplishments often nevertheless have high expectations in today's globalized world. The Global Current of Monoculture powerfully feeds dreams of Western-style material wealth among young Ugandans, dreams that have precious little chance of ever becoming reality. I heard the same observation from Samuel Wagaba, Isaac and Rebecca's twentysomething son who had survived dissolute teen years to become an itinerant youth evangelist.[7] In his ministry to youth, he said, he was encountering a generation of Ugandans disillusioned and resentful over not being able to enjoy the prosperity constantly depicted by media.

Damoni pointed out how Memory stokes the dysfunctional and manipulative relationship between Ugandans and foreign Christian workers. Several Ugandans discussed with me the open secret that every time Africans see Westerners, they think in terms of money and receiving. What a sad dance: well-meaning missionaries sacrificing comfort and money to share the gospel with compliant but impoverished Ugandans, who in turn listen patiently but often passively to the messages while waiting for the foreigners to bestow money.

Foreign workers sometimes honestly desire to see indigenous people assume leadership but encounter a dearth of qualified people with backgrounds in theology, preaching, or organizational leadership. It makes sense that many in Isaac Wagaba's and Damoni Kitabire's generations would be unpracticed at leading Christian organizations, after living under the rule of the British and having to go underground during the Obote and Amin regimes. The result can sometimes be inexperienced and immature leaders and shallow churches.

There is also another angle to Memory, where Christians and the global church not only inherit dysfunction, but make it worse. Foreign Christian workers play their part in the sad dance. Afforded honor and preeminence for more than a century, foreigners are often reluctant to share leadership with indigenous Christians. Because nationals have deferred to them, the missionaries have also become comfortable as pipers who call the tune but never occupy the second chair.

The disconnect is sometimes even comical, like the story of one encounter relayed by a friend who is a big-church American pastor—an informed, humble, lifelong student of the global church. Several years ago, he visited a prominent missionary who had lived in a town in Bangladesh for thirty years. He was driven through the desperately poor streets up to the missionary compound, where servants opened the gates to allow him in. As the gates closed and the car pulled into the drive, the missionary happily strode out to greet them. My friend recounted, "The sight of him took my breath away! He emerged from his large house onto the driveway, with servants milling all around in flowing saris and robes, in sandals or barefooted ... and there he stood—in a polyester red, white, and blue blazer, white belt and shoes, and pressed bright red slacks." Preserved from the press of humanity outside the gates, the man had lived for three decades without learning the language, let alone shedding his cruise leisurewear. The odds are that new missionaries in that village today must contend with perceptions of Christianity as foreign and uninterested in indigenous concerns or values. Like salt sewn into soil, the missionary's legacy lingers as a toxic element of that village's Memory.

Memory can be a trans-generational curse, and I have often wondered just how long it takes for formative past events to lose their hold on future people. I marvel at how the repressive forty-year reign of the Soviet Union continues to poison former Eastern Bloc countries over twenty years after the fall of the Iron Curtain in 1989. Even young people in Eastern Europe, who only know Communism from history books, cannot help but be infected by the attitudes and worldviews of parents who grew up in harsh, totalitarian homes and communities. So today, as the global church engages with Eastern European countries, it must recognize and account for pervasive isolation and distrust—of neighbors, classmates, coworkers, and even family.

I had not understood the deep psychological effect of the Soviet Union until I met with five brilliant young scholars who were studying at a think tank in Slovakia, the country that used to be the northern part of Czechoslovakia. They had come from Poland, Ukraine, and Russia to hone their intellectual and linguistic skills in preparation for leadership positions back home or abroad.

Their command of the English language and their familiarity with Western ways was astounding. I was fascinated, for four hours in a small back room of a Bratislava restaurant, to hear their current personal insights into post-Communist Eastern Europe.

Our discussion was wide-ranging and rich. Over a meal of goulash and noodles, we discussed global trends, changes in their native (former Soviet Union and Eastern Bloc) countries, and generational differences in worldview, customs, and cultures. As is so often the case with people around the world, these impressive young people delighted in answering question after question as I asked them about themselves and their countries. They also relished the chance to work on their English.

As our conversation neared its end, I asked them if they had more hope for the future than their parents had. Their responses stunned me. Or, I should say their lack of responses. For the first time that evening, their language skills abandoned them. Not just one, but all five graduate students stared at me blankly when I asked them about "hope."

It became clear that they only knew "hope" as a vocabulary word, a theory, and a virtue. These were Christians who felt confident of their eternal destiny, and that certainty provided them with long-term, philosophic hope and peace. As late twentysomethings who had grown up in Soviet societies, though, they had not successfully converted that intellectual certainty into personal hope and optimism. Their understanding of hope, it seemed, was forever colored and tainted by childhoods in toxic Soviet societies where parents kept secrets from children, children kept secrets from teachers and other classmates, and public lives never touched private lives.[8]

In so many countries, citizens bear the baggage of previous regimes and eras, which profoundly limits their ability or willingness to receive the gospel message. In countries dealing with this and other forms of Memory, what we see around us is not what we get; what lurks below the surface often counts for much more. The church's solution must not be to proclaim, publish, or pressure nonbelievers more insistently, for the invisible blockages created by Memory require different—not louder—approaches.

I have observed powerful ministries in Moscow that educate and train business owners about integrity, transparency, and accountability in their businesses. They teach, for instance, real-world principles in the Bible that discourage paying and receiving bribes. I have sat in on leadership courses in former Soviet countries, where Christian students associated leadership with oppression, domination, and power. The adept trainer was part business guru, part pastor, and part psychologist. In helping students to conceive that leaders might actually put the needs of others first, he presented Jesus and His loving Father as the ultimate examples of servant leadership. The teacher's effort to delink the images of authority figure and adversary was totally novel to the students, obviously the beginning of a long and complex process.

In their black trench coats, black blazers and shirts, and drainpipe black slacks, the three men in Kiev, Ukraine, were straight from central casting. There are characters like them—always the bad guys—in all Cold War spy movies. Here, though, they all worked for a premier Russian ministry and were my hosts during my time in Ukraine. One of them headed up the national office, and another was earning his PhD in philosophy and teaching apologetics to university students. Pavel was my translator, a gangly young father of three whose affability and charisma warmed up even the dreary Communist-era hotel lobby.

We started our chilly day strolling through Kiev's Pechersk Lavra. A lavra is a high-ranking monastery for Eastern Orthodox monks, with a church or refectory at the center. When it was founded in 1051, Pechersk Lavra was essentially a cluster of hilltop caves overlooking Kiev and the Dnieper River. Today its multiple gilded onion domes and maze of streets, alleys, and squares make it one of Kiev's major historical and architectural gems.

As we stood in the sacred square admiring the views and a nearby twelfth-century archway, a shiny, new black Mercedes SUV rumbled over the cobblestones. The vehicle surprised me, but not nearly so much as the driver—an old, long-bearded clergyman, in his black cassock, mitre hat, and dangling cross. The irony of the Orthodox priest, who lived in the Lavra as a servant of the Orthodox Church, driving the foreign luxury vehicle was completely lost on my hosts. One of them simply shrugged his shoulders and said, "You know that gift shop where you just bought those souvenirs—who do you think gets all that money?"

Distrust of authorities runs deep in Ukraine and in the former Soviet Union in general. The Christian church suffers from that legacy too, because it did not groom future leaders during Communist days. In Ukraine, as in most former Soviet Bloc countries, people recite a favorite saying: "The tree that stands tallest is cut down."[9]

Ukraine's prevailing skepticism toward leadership is a legacy of the autocratic, brutal Soviet rule—a classic case of the Global Current of Memory. Ukraine produced former premiers Leonid Brezhnev and Nikita Khrushchev, so associations with repressive men of power are relatively personal and recent. Living in a city that has been burned to the ground four times, citizens of Kiev are more resilient than trusting. In 1986, the Russian government initially covered up any news of the disastrous accident at the Chernobyl nuclear plant, even as the nuclear fallout was poisoning Ukrainians just sixty-eight miles north of Kiev. Finally, after seventy years of deception, betrayal, and oppression, in 1991 Ukraine was one of the first republics to break away from the Soviet Union.

Memory, like all Currents, seeps into and affects the church. As a result of the past, the Ukrainian church today lives with an inherited leadership vacuum. I met with many Ukrainian church leaders, and every one independently described the Ukrainian church's leadership void.

Dr. Gregory Komendant, the head of the Baptist Union in Ukraine, told me that the number of Baptist churches had increased from 900 to 2800 since 1991. American evangelist Franklin Graham held a public rally in Kiev in 2007 that 231,000 people attended. But this increase in the size of the flock only accentuated the urgent need for training, education, and mentoring of pastors and lay leaders.

Dr. Komendant himself was a vivid example of why mature, senior leaders were scarce in Ukraine. He and his peers had grown up in a society where Christians were discriminated against, persecuted, or punished. Christians and their families were denied educational and vocational opportunities. Dr. Komendant's baptism in 1968 had to be done at night and in secret. He recounted that his grandfather died while imprisoned for his faith. It is clear to see why few committed, dedicated leaders emerged out of that era.

Generations of repression and deprivation in Ukraine have taken their toll. That is Memory in action, and it is a main reason for Ukraine's current lack of mature Christian leaders. For decades there were no Ukrainian seminaries, so today's Ukrainian churches lack sophisticated, trained leaders. For seventy years during Soviet rule, Christians were kept in manual labor jobs and were not allowed beyond high school if they professed belief in God. Few Christians of prominence or wealth could protect or finance the Christian community, its seminaries, or the education of its leaders.

Some of Ukraine's Memory problems paralleled Uganda's quite closely. Ukrainians saw wealth on display in the thriving capital city of Kiev, but beyond some privileged urbanites, few others were sharing in that wealth. As in Uganda, this was causing a new form of dissatisfaction—far greater than that of Communist days when no one had any money and no one dared to expect a piece of the pie.

I was reminded of Damoni Kitabire and Samuel Wagaba's predictions of mounting frustration among youth in their country. In Uganda, the impediment to sharing in wealth was passivity, a legacy of postcolonialism and post-conflict. In Ukraine, the bar to wealth was often a weak work ethic, the remnant of a Communist economy that did not reward or encourage personal initiative. During Soviet years of centralized economic control, citizens joked about their Communist leaders, "They pretend to pay us, and we pretend to work."[10]

How should the global church respond as it encounters this type of Memory? First, the church must provide biblical teaching about money—contentment, envy, generosity, greed, and integrity—both for believers who have come into money and those who remain poor. Christian churches around the world must deal with rampant and crippling materialism, as globalization brings newfound wealth and prosperity in pockets. The global church must present an alternate, truly biblical paradigm to keep believers from replacing colonialism or Communism with materialism, individualism, and greed, as is already happening around the world.

The global church will have plentiful opportunities to minister everywhere in holistic ways—to serve both spiritual and physical needs. In

Ukraine, despite some appearances of prosperity, more than 40 percent of citizens live in poverty.[11] Worse still, Ukrainian citizens can no longer rely upon the old Soviet "safety net" of pay, vacation, health care, and retirement. This hits senior citizens especially hard, since they grew up assuming that the government would care for them in their later years, but that is proving not to be true.

Places like Ukraine are also experiencing the erosion of traditional family structures. Seventy percent of all pregnancies end in abortion there, they are facing one of the fastest growing HIV/AIDS epidemics in the world, and there are nearly one quarter of a million at-risk orphans and street children. Young adults are abandoning parents and grandparents for better opportunities elsewhere. The church will have plentiful opportunities for developing ministries that serve families—including counseling in former Soviet countries where the very idea of counseling was ridiculed for decades.

Later in the afternoon, Pavel led us on a walking tour of Kiev's rolling hills overlooking the Dnieper River, to the Museum of the Great Patriotic War of 1941–45. There we encountered a memorial park filled with tanks, missiles, bomber jets, cannons, and acres of sculptures. No matter where I travel in countries with Communist pasts, the sculptures are always the same: blocky, massive, testosterone-infused depictions of military might and societal unity. Nothing says unity, apparently, like soldiers, scientists, and engineers surging out of the fields and into the fray. The massive Mao monument in the center of Shenyang, China features a cluster on the base, including a girl in pigtails, an apron-wearing, pistol-brandishing mom, and an opium-smoking grandfather charging together toward some unknown foe. Sign me up!

In Kiev, the most prominent and poignant statue is the Motherland Monument. She stands, all 530 tons, on a hill visible throughout Kiev. In 1981, then-Soviet leader Leonid Brezhnev dedicated the statue, along with a nearby "Flame of Glory" to blaze in perpetuity in honor of Soviet bravery. I noted that there was no longer a flame burning in the elevated cement bowl the size of a baseball diamond. I did not miss the irony of a perpetual "Flame of Glory" without any fire.

As I stood there, a nearby English-speaking guide was talking to her tour group. To my ears, she was providing a crystal clear explanation of Memory. As part of the ongoing two-decade battle over access and control of the region's natural resources, she said, Russia was currently rationing natural gas levels to Ukraine. That, she noted, was why the flame was extinguished. If I had been a businessman on that tour, my mind would immediately have gravitated to issues like how that would affect my gas costs, whether there would be frequent interruptions of electricity, whether the gas squabble means danger for residents, whether anti-Ukrainian sentiment in the future might hinder efforts to generate business in Russia, and more. All are issues of Memory.

We in the global church should practice information arbitrage just as ardently as businesspeople, constantly considering how to adapt our approaches for changing societies and individuals. Tried and true formulas are not adequate for the global church, any more than best practices from Soviet times are adequate for today's Kiev businessmen and women. Glorifying and enjoying God in these times of constant white water—that is a challenge that requires the flexibility of Apple Guy and the resolve of Mission Marm.

Memory

Representative Organizations

Memory is an easy Global Current to overlook and a difficult one for finding a distinctively Christian or biblical response. For that reason, the sources of best practices in dealing with Memory are not aggressive ministries but reflective think tanks, educational institutions, and publishers. This is all the more reason for the global church to find a way to minister actively to lingering hurts and pain while also charting a hopeful way forward. Following are great sources of information for relating to people struggling with the lingering effects of Memory.

1. **Duke Center for Reconciliation:** The Center for Reconciliation at Duke Divinity School inspires, forms, and supports leaders, communities, and congregations to live as ambassadors of reconciliation. The Center's leaders, Ugandan Emmanuel Katongole and American Chris Rice, have personally seen Memory in action during years in East Africa and the American South. The Center flows from the apostle Paul's affirmation in 2 Corinthians 5 that, through Christ, "the message of reconciliation has been entrusted to us." (www.divinity.duke.edu/reconciliation/index.html)

2. **L'Abri England:** Marsh Moyle is a British-born scholar who ran CityGate in Bratislava, Slovakia, before he became Missionary in Residence at L'Abri England. During more than two decades in the former Soviet Union, Moyle dedicated himself to helping post-Soviet Eastern Europeans bridge the gap between the reality of Christ and everyday life. For over fifty years, those people had been told that the Party was the answer to all their needs and that

religion had no place in society. Moyle understands culture and produces scholarship that especially speaks to leaders—Christian and non-Christian—with high education and high learning potential. (www.labri.org/england/index.html and www.citygate.org)

3. **Lead Consulting**: Lead Consulting is a Raleigh, North Carolina, publisher of books that assist people throughout the world in their spiritual journeys. One of their writers, Ralph Ennis, is director of Intercultural Training and Research for The Navigators ministry. I learned about Ennis, who has been studying and writing about intercultural issues for more than two decades, through his remarkable little booklet, *An Introduction to the Mainland Chinese Soul.* A Chinese scholar wrote, "Deceptively simple and straightforward in its presentation, ... its perceptive analysis of Chinese attitudes toward spiritual matters not only reveals the obstacles to sharing one's faith within the Chinese context but also points out natural bridges of understanding that span cultural differences."[12] (www.leadconsulting-usa.com)

4. **Geert Hofstede Cultural Dimensions:** In 1967, IBM Corporation hired Professor Geert Hofstede, a Dutch writer internationally recognized for his studies of national cultures. From 1967 to 1973, Hofstede collected data from employees in seventy countries and developed the Geert-Hofstede scale to show how cultural values affect workplace dynamics. It scores countries in five different areas, including tolerance for ambiguity, gender differentiation, individualism, distribution of power, and long-term orientation.[13] (www.geert-hofstede.com)

Conclusion

A Changing of the Guard

Quite inexplicably, I was invited to a conference in Austin, Texas for Christian hipsters. I mentioned this to my brother-in-law, Greg—a fantastic guy and Austinite who at the time had a waist-length pony tail. He was amused. I could tell he had serious doubts about how hip a conference could be if I were invited.

In truth, I attended the Q Conference in Austin's ornate Paramount Theatre just to get a feel for the young men and women who will play lead roles in the global church in coming years. It all made me very hopeful.

This was an Apple Guy conference. The NextGen buzzwords were flying: culture, community, context, relevance, transcendence, authenticity, incarnation, sustainability, mercy, and justice. They talked about their stories, their narratives, their arcs. The men wore jeans with shirttails untucked. Many of them had soul patches or goatees, with lots of shaved heads, spiked hair, or surfer bangs. Piercings and tattoos, too—gender non-specific.

I was not the oldest person in attendance, but the oldest folks would have been seniors when I was a freshman. The few middle-agers definitely stood out. Besides our looks, we older folks had another commonality: We were all in leadership positions with formal Christian organizations. This concerned me greatly. Compared to the rest of the crowd, we looked so white, Western, and weathered.

I realized, in Austin, that I am at risk of being a 2010 version of Mission Marm. I have not spent my life in the jungles of the global south, but I *have* been hibernating for thirty years, Rip Van Winkle-like, in the heart of the American Christian subculture. I can easily see how Mission Marm, reentering into a globalizing world after decades away, might find the Meeting of the Waters to be confusing and even troubling. And how she might wrestle with indecision, unsure whether to trust finely honed instincts and rely on peers in her traditional stream or to look toward new, untested streams of great promise.

At one of the conference's breakout sessions of about fifty people, a middle-aged man had a few questions for the group. He worked for a Christian radio station, and he asked for a show of hands of everyone who watched Christian television. No hands went up, which did not deter him, because he was most interested in the follow-up question: "How many of you listen to Christian radio?" Again, radio silence. Then a couple of hands inched up, and the people admitted that they sometimes listened to Christian radio when their children were in the car. Finally, he asked, "How many listen to National Public Radio?" This time about three-quarters of the hands shot up. The message was stark: Christian radio, such a mainstay during the last half of the twentieth century, might be facing some nasty future demographics. People under forty had deserted newspapers and network television a decade earlier, and now it appeared that they might similarly be deserting mainstream Christian radio.

Christian radio now had to come to grips with the separate and parallel stream, not currently being reached, of radically changing listening habits. The new stream, characterized by the unbridled vigor, youth, and momentum I saw at Q, was self-consciously "other" and offered no obvious points of access. This was not just a developing trend, but a new dynamic that was established and making waves.

As attitudes toward radio and other Christian media shift, the Global Currents help us isolate and name just what propels those movements. As a prism separates a single source of light into seven separate colors (red, orange, yellow, green, blue, indigo, and violet), the Currents provide seven angles from which to approach and assess different cultures and contexts facing the global church. For the Christian radio industry, that kind of deep understanding will be the necessary first step toward relevancy to younger generations of Christians around the world. Such an analysis would include the following observations:

- Mercy—The Mercy Generation, with such an emphasis on acts of service, can be expected to shy away from mass-proclamation vehicles like radio.

- Migration—Young Christians live in ethnically diverse, pluralistic settings and are very comfortable with secular information sources outside of the Christian "bubble."

- Machines—Technological tools like MP3 players, social-network Web sites, blogs, and digital readers allow personalized media and instant, streaming access to breaking news,[1] instead of packaged and labeled news or old mass media like mainstream radio.

- Mediation—Younger Christians may bristle against the monolithic, us-versus-them impression that Christian radio and other mass media can project.

Our goal is always to present the gospel in fresh ways—in our homes, churches, workplaces, and areas of ministry. By continually tracking the Currents, we can notice incremental blips that may add up to major shifts. This kind of vigilance will be crucial to ministry workers in the coming era of the global church, as we move into the hearts of our cities or travel to far-flung places for short periods of time. The Currents are tools for navigating constant, dizzying change with more cultural discernment and alertness, enabling Apple Guy and his peers to steer the global church downstream, beyond the Meeting of the Waters.

Mission Marm did not face the same challenges, and she did not need the same set of skills. First, she did not live in a world of constant change, so she did not need a tool like the Global Currents for ongoing adaptation. Second, her commitment to missions was for a lifetime, so she would have quite a while to work things out. Quick adaptation was not a major concern. Finally, her focus was local and not global, since she bade farewell to the events and goings-on of the broader world when she committed to a life in the field.

Homer and Edith Moser heard God's call in 1921 and became Presbyterian missionaries to Brazil. They were the first people from their Ohio county to "go abroad." As they prepared for their deployment to the jungles of Brazil, they probably never met a Brazilian person or heard one speak. All they saw of their new home was in grainy, black-and-white photographs.

Homer was affable and enterprising, Edith driven and indomitable. They brought to Brazil the backbreaking work ethic they had learned growing up on Mennonite farms. Their mission agency purchased a large piece of barren land in Buriti, Brazil, far from the nearest town. While many missionaries started elementary schools, the Mosers opened a boarding high school for very poor rural children who had no access to public education. They were ambitious, aiming to equip all students for leadership in their homes, churches, and communities.

The Mosers innovated in many ways. Homer started growing pineapples, which had not previously been introduced to that region but soon grew quite prolifically. Edith made bricks from clay and straw and personally designed and oversaw construction of an elegant church. Homer put in place an elaborate plumbing system with bamboo pipes, in a region that had no electricity or running water. Edith taught classical piano to the students, though she had never touched the instrument before arriving in Brazil. Through it all, they grew followers of Christ.[2]

The fruit of their time in Brazil was abundant, if unglamorous and slow. Their boarding school progeny went on to noble and notable positions, as pastors, doctors, missionaries, a world-class musician, and a professor at Latin America's largest private university. Of their five biological children, Homer and Edith tragically buried Bobby, their firstborn son, in Buriti after he succumbed to tropical disease. Happily for me, their second daughter, Marjory, later became my mom.

It was forty-six years before the Mosers returned to the United States. During that time, they did what Mission Marms did best: They served, and they stayed. The Mosers experienced the fullness of a call well-answered. Everything about them—their preparation, their methods, and their longevity—was a product of their times.

It could not happen that way today. Foreign assignments are more restrictive and ever tightening for Christian workers, in Brazil and in many countries around the world. In Brazil, for instance, the government is increasingly concerned about protecting its indigenous tribes (often called "first peoples") from outside influences. Generally, the Brazilian government is resistant to American involvement, from medical aid and supplies to missionaries. In the twenty-first century, the Brazilian government has become stingier about allowing new missionaries into the country and has even revoked existing missionary visas. The Currents have shifted, and the church must respond.

In today's political environment, an entrenched American couple thoroughly assimilated into the culture and life of the Brazilian interior would cause considerable heartburn for Brazilian officials. If the Mosers were serving in Brazil today, it is most likely that the government would eventually require them to leave or would tighten restrictions so that leaving would be their only bearable choice. Without the Mosers, though, the government would still wish to continue the missionary-run boarding schools, which have long provided excellent education to otherwise-overlooked Brazilian children. The next step would be to offer limited-duration missionary visas to the Mosers' replacements, with considerable restrictions on their travel and ministry scope.

Which brings us back to Apple Guy. Brazil's tightening restrictions are exactly why Apple Guy came through the missionary bunkhouse in Manaus, heading to the boarding school in the Brazilian interior. He was replacing people just like Homer and Edith Moser, long-termers who were either completing their tenure or who had been rousted out by new government restrictions. He was moving his family to answer a calling in their lives, which was a plenty serious act. I suspect, though, that if he had known what a critical role he would play in steering the global church beyond the Meeting of the Waters, it might have scared him senseless. I admit that it still concerns me today.

As between Mission Marm and Apple Guy, this is not a story about laggards or leaders, right or wrong. Rather it is the story of artisans who have worked lovingly and excellently on a grand cathedral for their whole lives and who are now handing the task over to a younger generation to work on the next stage. The pioneers might have laid the foundation, for instance, and the successors will build the ceiling or windows or even the spire—so a very different set of skills will be required. Different generations are used by God to serve the world in different ways at different times.

Today's global church would not be so vibrant and robust were it not for Mission Marm. At the same time, the global church of tomorrow will not thrive unless fellow Christians embrace and God empowers Apple Guy and his peers. They will need supernatural doses of adaptability and relevance as well as biblical orthodoxy. Those need to be the unique hallmarks of the global church's next generation.

Those of us who wish to be part of the Christian church's future need to be like the group of men that gave support to newly crowned King David in the Old Testament (1 Chron. 12:32). The sons of Isaachar were the smallest group in number, but they brought uncommon wisdom. A commentator describes them as possessing "an understanding of public affairs, the temper of the nation, and the tendencies of the present events."[3] The global church needs just such people at the helm.

Christianity around the world, too often viewed as staid or boring or regressive, actually provides the richest journey that life can offer. The people are riveting, the issues compelling, and the stakes high. God knows the future beyond the Meeting of the Waters is full of possibility, hope, and reward—and the world is waiting … but not for long.

Acknowledgments

For years I've had the privilege of meeting with great leaders of the global Church. My job has been part Larry King and part Christian fantasy camp. I could not possibly list the thousands of ministry leaders, from a hundred nations, who patiently allowed me to pick their brains, but I am deeply grateful to each of them.

Some brave publishing pros took a flyer on me, a first-time author. I can unreservedly say that this book would never have seen the light of day without John Eames, my best literary ally and a good friend. I especially appreciated Don Pape's unbridled enthusiasm and confidence at David C. Cook Publishing. Laid-back John Blase was the right editor to work with such a hyper-engaged (my kids call it obsessive-compulsive) author. Also, Cook's team of Ingrid Beck, Amy Kiechlen, Douglas Mann, Amy Quicksall, Angie Ralston, and Caitlyn York all made big differences in this book.

A cloud of witnesses has truly aided the writing of this book. I received critical (in both meanings of the word) feedback from a handful of people who were generous with their time and discerning eyes: Dave Clarke, Andy Crouch, Patrick Hiltz, Peter Jones, Val Kling, Blaine Lay, Adrianne Thompson, and George Walker. All helped to make this a better book and bolstered me more than they know.

I am grateful for friends who, in their unique ways, gave me significant boosts along the way: Stacy Adams, Anjum Khurshid and Hadi Yazdanpanah,

James and Dodie Anderson, Zack Aspegren, David Baer, David Bailey, Beth Baleke, Charles Beckett, Nicole Benham, Lindsay Brown, Ben Campbell, Rudy Carrasco, J. G. and Jill Carter, Tom and Nancy Chewning, Pam Clarke, Don Coleman, Chuck Colson and the Centurions program, Michelle Conn, Don Costello, Imad Damaj, Anita Deyneka, Listwella Donaldson, Mark Dozier, Audrey and Jim Duval, Don Eberly, Ben Edwards, Brian Edwards, Ali Faruk, John Featherston, David Fleming, Howard Freeman, Abi and Ryan Frederick, Andrew Fuller, D. J. Glisson, Eddy Gonzalez, Joe Gouverneur, Aaron Graham, Os Guinness, Hamad, Richard Haney, Chris Heuertz, James Hildebrand, Kay Hiramine, Billy Hoffman, Michael Jaffarian, Gary Jennings, Andrew Jones, John Keltonic, Dan Kennedy, Rich Keshian, Annette and Malik Khan, Peter Kuzmic, Mark Labberton, David Livermore, Rick Love, Allan Matamouros, Charles and Susan Mendies, Hugo Morales, Virginia and Darrell Morrow, Jana Muntsinger, Bob Muzikowski, Mac Myers, Ken and Linda Newsome, Minh Ha Nguyen, Scott Oostdyk, Nelson and Lisa Ould, Dan Palazzolo, Becca Parker, Caroline Harmon Peery, Paul Pierson, Gay and Vernon Plack, Kara Powell, Vinay Samuel, Rick Schofield, Bob Seiple, Steve Shaffer, Becky and Tim Shah, Joe Slay, Fred Smith, Harold Smith, Mark Sprinkle, Todd Stephens, Lynn and Mark Valeri, Tonya Venuti, George Verwer, Cricket White, Scott White, Corey Widmer, Steve Woodrow, Third Presbyterian's young adult class, and my mom, Marjory Robertson. And I owe so much to my friends in the foundation world: brilliant folks and good people, they welcomed me years ago as a neophyte, shared insights and methods, and modeled collegiality.

As I worked on *The Meeting of the Waters* for over five years, I learned that authoring is a very solitary process. It was refreshing, along the way, then, to be known by a few others, whether they showed bewilderment, expressed curiosity, or simply talked trash about my secret writing life. I know that success has many fathers, but failure is an orphan. If this book tanks, all blame rightfully points to me. If the book thrives, and God uses it for good, the people named above deserve kudos.

Notes

Introduction:

1. *The American Heritage Dictionary of the English Language,* 4th ed., s.v. "Schoolmarm."

2. "And He was saying to them all, 'If anyone wishes to come after Me, he must deny himself, and take up his cross daily, and follow Me.'" (Luke 9:23 NASB) "Go therefore and make disciples of all the nations, baptizing them in the name of the Father and the Son and the Holy Spirit … and lo, I am with you always, even to the end of the age." (Matt. 28:19–20 NASB)

3. Stan Guthrie, *Missions in the Third Millennium: 21 Key Trends for the 21st Century* (Carlisle, UK: Paternoster Press, 2005), 162.

4. Bernice Martin, "A New Evangelism for the US," *TimesOnline,* April 16, 2008, http://entertainment.timesonline.co.uk/tol/arts_and_entertainment/the_tls/article3757543.ece.

5. More specifically, in 2000 there were 419,524 Christian foreign missionaries serving outside of their own countries. This figure includes Protestant, Independent, Anglican, Roman Catholic, and Orthodox Christians. *World Christian Encyclopedia: A Comparative Survey of Churches and Religions in the Modern World,* 2nd ed., ed. David B. Barrett, George T. Kurian, and Todd M. Johnson (Oxford: Oxford University Press, 2001), 1:843.

6. Lausanne Committee for World Evangelism, "Globalization and the Gospel: Rethinking Mission in the Contemporary World," Lausanne Occasional Paper No. 30 (September 29–October 5, 2004).

7. Tatiana Simonian, *Anthem,* May/June 2006, 35.

8. Vadim Kotelnikov, "Case Study: General Electric (GE)—Creating an Extraordinary Organization," 1000ventures.com, http://www.1000ventures.com/ business_guide/cs_inex_ge.html.

9. John Stott, *The Contemporary Christian* (Downers Grove, IL: InterVarsity, 1992), 13. "I believe we are called to the difficult and even painful task of 'double listening.' That is, we are to listen carefully … both to the ancient Word and to the modern world, in order to relate the one to the other with a combination of fidelity and sensitivity … only if we can develop our capacity for double listening, will we avoid the opposite pitfalls of unfaithfulness and irrelevance, and be able to speak God's Word to God's world with effectiveness today." In his review of *The World is Flat*, Bill Yarbrough writes, "But when a longing for the past defines how we approach missions we can become blind or oblivious to the changing cultural and sociological dynamics around us. Even worse, we can become detached from the mass movements of peoples, thought, and ideas that swirl around the walls of our evangelical fortresses" (*InVision*, December 2005, http://www.mtw.org/home/site/templates/mtw_invision. asp?_resolutionfile=templatespath%7Cmtw_invision.asp&area_2=public/ Resources/Invision/2005/12/ReviewWorldFlat).

10. Thomas Friedman, *The Lexus and the Olive Tree* (New York: Anchor Books, 1999), 20. Friedman quotes Yale international-relations historians Paul Kennedy and John Lewis Gaddis as they explain why a generalist view of the world is most helpful:

> "The dominant trend within universities and the think tanks is toward ever-narrower specialization: A higher premium is placed on functioning deeply within a single field than broadly across several. And yet without some awareness of the whole—without some sense of how means converge to accomplish or to frustrate ends—there can be no strategy. And without strategy, there is only drift."

Innovation expert Frans Johansson notes that nowadays most major achievements involve combining concepts between multiple fields, "generating ideas that leap in new directions." That applies to scientists, to journalists, and even to farmers. "These days, farmers are expected to be expert meteorologists, agronomists, and environmentalists. Oh, and by the way, they have to be expert traders, too," said Warren Staley, CEO of agricultural giant Cargill, the US' largest private company (Franz Johansson, *The Medici Effect* [Boston: Harvard Business School Publishing, 2004], 31). Information arbitrage is equally essential for world-class journalists, creative-types, and CEOs of large organizations.

Information arbitrage is also necessary for everybody who plays a part in, or cares about, missions. Missionaries can arbitrage in their day-to-day interactions by considering multiple aspects of the lives of both themselves and their indigenous friends. They can see beyond their traditional areas of interaction such as Bible studies and teaching, to "read the connections, and connect the dots." Laypeople at home can arbitrage as they read the daily news or read prayer letters. Theologian Karl Barth recommended information arbitrage when he said that Christians should live each day with a newspaper in one hand and a Bible in the other.

This approach may be uneasy territory for many mission-driven people of faith. It may seem offensive to talk about evangelism and the gospel in the same breath as IBM, *The Lexus and the Olive Tree,* and the CEOs of Cargill and General Electric. But I am not urging anyone to question the gospel or its truth, but instead to question the way the gospel is communicated to people of other cultures. Borrowing principles from other fields (business, economics, sociology, marketing, etc.) is not an effort to replace God's power and grace in reaching the lost, but rather an effort to equip missionaries to communicate the gospel, in the most effective way possible, to the people of their day.

The concept of information arbitrage could not be more timely for the mission enterprise. Now is a time when strong leadership is needed regarding how missions should adapt to our world in the twenty-first century, with all of the challenges and opportunities of globalization.

Chapter 1

1. I read a missionary letter written by "JPL" on February 13, 2006 with a delightful entry called "The Last Forty Kilometers," which described the jet lag and physical fatigue—and the even more difficult culture shock—faced by such travelers: "Newcomers to our city discover soon enough that the seventeen-hour trans-Atlantic flight, taxing as it may be, is not really the greatest leap of all. The urban world of southern Africa is in many ways close cultural kin to the other great cities of the planet—a world of reinforced concrete, of cell phones, crime, newspapers, supermarkets, Hollywood icons and paved parking lots.

No, the greatest leap, in terms of culture, comes about forty kilometers from our city center. Across that divide is where vertigo and culture-lag really begin to take hold."

2. Andy Crouch, "Experiencing Life at the Margins," *Christianity Today,* July 2006. Sociologists call this intercultural engagement—the process of trying to reach people of other nationalities and cultures. I talked to a friend who is a scholar in intercultural engagement about the best way to understand foreign, unfamiliar cultures. For several decades, in his capacity as a staff trainer with the Navigators ministry, Ralph Ennis has researched and written on bridging cultures. Though delivered in his soft North Carolina drawl, Ralph's response could have come straight from Rev. Dr. David Zac Niringiye's mouth. He said that what is required is a "come and see" approach to engaging with people of other cultures.

3. Trends of globalization have been the intense focus of business, military, education, and government leaders around the world. Every week a new book, periodical, or news report provides a fresh take on globalization's all-consuming swath. The church world, though, has been tentative and inconsistent in approaching the Currents. That must change if the global church is to remain effective in our all-bets-are-off world.

4. Michael Jaffarian, "Globalization and the American Missions Movement" (presentation to the Evangelical Fellowship of Mission Agencies Executive Retreat, September 2006).

5. Mark Twain, *Life on the Mississippi* (New York: Bantam Books, 1945), 64–65. Twain elaborates, "I think a pilot's memory is about the most wonderful thing in the world. To know the Old and New Testament by heart, and be able to recite them glibly, forward or backward, or begin at random anywhere in the book and recite both ways and never trip or make a mistake, is no extravagant mass of knowledge, and no marvelous facility, compared to a pilot's massed knowledge of the Mississippi and his marvelous facility in the handling of it. I make the comparison deliberately, and believe I am not expanding the truth when I do it. Many will think my figure too strong, but pilots will not."

6. Friedman, *The Lexus and the Olive Tree*, 20.

7. Friedman borrows this concept from the financial world, where arbitrage is the purchase of products in one market and the sale of them in another for a

profit. Arbitrage is a method used to make money by investors with detailed knowledge of different markets around the world, who play the different markets off of one another to make a profit.

> [T]he key to being a successful arbitrageur is having a wide net of informants and information and then knowing how to synthesize it in a way that will produce a profit. If you want to be an effective reporter or columnist trying to make sense of global affairs today, you have to be able to do something similar.... To be an effective foreign affairs columnist or reporter, you have to learn how to arbitrage information from these disparate perspectives and then weave it all together to produce a picture of the world that you would never have if you looked at it from only one perspective. That is the essence of information arbitrage.

Chapter 2

1. Norimitsu Onishi, "Tension, Desperation: The China-North Korean Border," *New York Times,* October 22, 2006.
2. Open Doors, "World Watch List 2009," http://www.opendoorsusa.org/content/view/432.
3. Bruce Falconer, "The World in Numbers: Murder by the State," *Atlantic Monthly,* November 2003, 56–57.
4. Frederick Buechner, *Wishful Thinking: A Theological ABC* (New York: Harper & Row, 1973), 95.
5. David Kinnaman and Gabe Lyons, *unChristian: What a New Generation Really Thinks about Christianity ... and Why It Matters* (Grand Rapids, MI: Baker Books, 2007), 23.
6. President of the Barna Group Dave Kinnaman qualifies, "[I]dentifying a 'generation' is an analytical tool for understanding our culture and the people within it. It simply reflects the idea that people who are born over a certain period of time are influenced by a unique set of circumstances and global events, moral and social values, technologies, and cultural and behavioral norms. The result is that every generation has a different way of seeing life.

Recognizing the generational concept as a tool, rather than as definitive for every person, means that exceptions are to be expected" (*unChristian*, 17).

7. Howard Fineman, "Our New Tribes," *Newsweek*, January 26, 2009, 61.

8. *Stanford Social Innovation Review* 6.3 (2008).

9. Bob Roberts, Jr., *Glocalization: How Followers of Jesus Engage a Flat World* (Grand Rapids, MI: Zondervan, 2007), 139. This issue has been the focus of extensive writing and debate. An excellent article by Scott Abbleby and Angela Lederach compares two approaches to evangelism, the "Witness" mode and the "Conversion" mode. The Witness mode involves sharing the gospel in explicit biblical terms but refusing to separate the theological from the social. The Witness approach may be theologically troubling to many Christians more accustomed to the Conversion mode, which serves God solely by spreading the good news of salvation in order to convert people to Christianity ("Conversion, Witness, Solidarity, Dialogue: Modes of the Evangelizing Church in Tension," *The Review of Faith and International Affairs* 1 [Spring 2009]: 11). I believe that, in practice, distinctions between the various modes of evangelism are often unclear, especially as evangelism is practiced in wildly different locales around the world. I also see the Mercy Generation as being more fragmented and nuanced than preceding generations, too complex for casual theological categorization.

10. Tim Keller, "Evangelistic Worship," June 2001, http://download.redeemer. com/pdf/learn/resources/Evangelistic_Worship-Keller.pdf.

11. Gary Haugen, interview by Stan Guthrie, "Pivoting Toward the Faraway Neighbor," *Christianity Today*, January 2009, 34–35.

12. Kinnaman and Lyons, *unChristian*, 23.

13. "Inclusive Leadership Motivates X and Y," Robert Half International, media release, July 2005.

14. John Stonestreet, "Why Students Don't 'Get It,'" *Truth & Consequences*, June 2009.

15. "India," Operation World, November 2, 2008, http://www.operationworld. org/country/indi/owtext.html.

16. "North Korea Famine," *Wikipedia*, http://en.wikipedia.org/wiki/North_Korean _famine.

17. "Korea, Democratic People's Republic," World Food Programme, http://www. wfp.org/countries/korea-democratic-peoples-republic-dprk.

18. Percentage of Christians provided by my host, who said that his survey contained the most reliable data available at the time in that intensely secretive country. Population estimate: Tom O'Neill, "Escape from North Korea," *National Geographic,* February 2009, 74.

19. "Open Doors Requests Urgent Prayer for North Korea," *Frontline Faith,* March 2008.

Chapter 3:

1. Lausanne presents six recommendations for intercultural cooperation between Christians from different parts of the world: (1) All international partnerships should exist primarily for the benefit of local congregations, not parachurch or international religious organizations. Thus, the first question that should be asked is: "How will missionary efforts impact local Christians?" (2) Non-resident missionaries and humanitarian workers should serve as positive models of intercultural cooperation. All too often, mission and service organizations function as independent entities instead of working in partnership with local Christians. Those outside the Christian community learn volumes from the example of Christians from different cultures who are able to cooperate with each other in mutual respect. Creative partnerships need to emerge in which missionaries see themselves as learners and beneficiaries and not simply as those who are coming to give and direct. (3) Mission and service agencies should assist at the point of greatest need as defined by local residents. The external priorities of Westerners should not carry more weight in decision making than the views of those who live in Central Asia. (4) Programs should be long-term, not temporary, token gestures that cannot be sustained. (5) All international initiatives should be rooted in the specific cultural context of the region, cultural sensitivity being the foundation for effective partnerships. (6) Christian missionaries and service workers participating in inter-church partnerships must be vigilant to conduct their dealings with complete ethical and financial integrity. (A. Christian van Gorder, *Muslim-Christian Relations in Central Asia,* [London: Routledge, 2008], 95.)

2. Jenny Taylor, "Taking Spirituality Seriously: Northern Uganda and Britain's 'Break the Silence' Campaign," *The Round Table* 94.382 (October 2005), 562–63.

3. Joe Nam, "Orombi entourage weep on tour of Pabbo camp in Northern Uganda," *New Vision Newspaper,* March 8, 2004.

4. Long deputized as the army and police force during Uganda's six decades (1896–1962) as a British protectorate, the Acholis brought to the table a desire for some sort of reparation—and a propensity for conflict. Indeed, all of northern Uganda had a long-standing adversarial and suspicious relationship with the national government down in Kampala, feeling that President Museveni and his army had preyed upon northerners for years.

5. North Ugandans were suspicious that the indictments were largely an effort by Europeans to galvanize support for the ICC's future, since the young body was just created in 2002. Further, the United States under George W. Bush had withdrawn support of the ICC, and the last thing that the Europeans wanted was to see Bush's agenda prevail.

6. Zachary Lomo, "Why the International Criminal Court must withdraw Indictments against the Top LRA Leaders: A Legal Perspective," *The Sunday Monitor,* August 2006.

7. "If they decide that the best way to deal with their past is to forgive all those who have committed crimes against civilians, that wish has to be respected by others, including the ICC. If they decide that those who were responsible for the violation of human rights should be dealt with in accordance with their own traditions, that too has to be respected by all who do not share the values of the people affected.... [J]ustice is not just about trying, convicting, and sentencing those who have committed crimes to prison in order to appease those who suffered as a result of the actions of the accused. That is avenging the dead. True justice must first and foremost ensure that those alive can continue living in dignity and security. That requires a far more holistic approach than the self-righteous one of the ICC and its supporters (namely fixing the bad guys). The latter approach is both simplistic and mechanistic, if not superficial and fails to address the root causes which are both internal and external." (Ibid.) I also read a fascinating article on traditional Acholi approaches to justice and reconciliation, which are night-and-day different from the model I studied in law school (Joanna Quinn, "Beyond Truth Commissions: Indigenous Reconciliation in Uganda," *The Review of Faith and International Affairs* 4.1 [2006]: 31–37).

8. In one newspaper interview, he explained, "If you are [an Acholi] father and your child is abducted, then two years later, you see his dead body in a

newspaper with the caption, 'Ugandan Army Kills Thirty Rebels,' how would you feel?" (Joe Nam, "Orombi entourage weep on tour of Pabbo camp in Northern Uganda," *The New Vision Newspaper,* March 8, 2004). He railed against the world's indifference to the crisis for so long, chastising newspaper editors, "Don't just report rebels, rebels, rebels. Tell human stories. Tell the stories of these kids." (Taylor, "Taking Spirituality Seriously," 567.)

9. Zac continued, "What was done to [Zimbabwe's tyrant] Charles Taylor—buy him out. We need to work at identifying one or two countries which are open to considering the possibility of [allowing Kony to live there in exile]." (Ibid, 570.)

10. Andy Crouch, "Experiencing Life at the Margins," *Christianity Today,* July 2006.

11. A British scholar wrote, "The Ugandan Church uses religion to make new spaces for dialogue and new ways of transcending the crisis. Only the Church is simultaneously there on the ground, close enough to the people and their world-view, yet able to access international mechanisms of justice ... [giving] wide cross-cultural access to the reality of Acholi suffering. Northern Uganda is as a result less invisible, less remote." ("Taking Spirituality Seriously," 571.)

12. Crouch, "Experiencing Life at the Margins."

13. In *The Changing Face of World Missions,* authors Michael Pocock, Gailyn Van Rheenen, and Douglas McConnell write, "The Roman and Greek empires spread far beyond their points of origin, taking their ideas, innovations, and systems of governance with them. Islamic faith and culture spread widely around the Mediterranean world after AD 732, and the Mongol Empire spread from Mongolia into China and across Asia to Vienna by 1241. In South America, the Incas established an empire covering what today are several nation-states, and the Spanish, English, and French became dynamic catalysts for the spread of commerce, culture, and religion over extended areas of the world from 1500 onward. Historically, empires expanded outward from the center: Over the course of history, centers have included Athens, Rome, Beijing, Cuzco, Seville and London." ([Grand Rapids, MI: Baker Academic, 2005], 23.)

14. "Global south" is a term that originated in academic circles, as an improvement on other designations viewed as outdated, insensitive, or incorrect. "Third world" was deemed outdated, having been coined in 1952 to refer

to countries during the Cold War that were neither aligned with Capitalist NATO (first world) nor the Communist Soviet Bloc (second world). Another problem is that third world refers to political or economic divisions and is not as precise when used to describe social conditions. Third world economies typically shared traits of dependence upon exportation of primary products to the first and second worlds, overpopulation, low literacy rates, political instability, and immature industrial and technological sectors. Some experts disapprove of the terms "developing countries" and "underdeveloped countries"; they suggest such designations are derogatory and imply that industrialization is the only progressive way. Therefore, many prefer "two-thirds world" (because two-thirds of the world is underdeveloped). For the same apparent reason, an article I recently read used the term "four-fifths world." ("Third World," *Wikipedia*, http://en.wikipedia.org/wiki/Third_World.)

15. The term is extremely ambiguous, though, and in some contexts it can also include Australia and New Zealand and even Japan and South Korea, which are all members of the Organization for Economic Co-operation and Development (OECD) along with European Union (EU) nations. These are Western European or Western European-settled nations that enjoy relatively strong economies and stable governments, have chosen democracy as a form of governance, favor capitalism and free international trade, and have some form of political and military alliance or cooperation. When people in mission circles talk about "the West" or "Western countries," they are always referring to Western Europe, the United States, and Canada, and sometimes to Latin America, Australia, and New Zealand. ("Western World," *Wikipedia*, http://en.wikipedia.org/wiki/Western_world.)

16. Philip Jenkins, *The Next Christendom: The Coming of Global Christianity* (Oxford: Oxford University Press, 2002).

17. Political speechwriter Michael Gerson referred to "the intense, irrepressible Christianity of the global south." (Michael Gerson, "Missionaries in Northern Virginia," *Washington Post*, May 16, 2007, A15.)

18. India Missions Agency Annual Reports, Financial Year 2006-2007 (presented at Annual General Meeting, Dehradun, India, May 3, 2007).

19. Chris Wright, "An Upside-Down World," *Christianity Today*, January 18, 2007, http://www.christianitytoday.com/ct/2007/january/30.42.html.

20. Dr. David Wesley, induction address, Winter 2006, http://www.nts.edu/induction-address-dr-david-wesley-winter-2006.

21. In 2008, "on average, actively religious donors gave considerably more to charitable causes than other donors surveyed. The average total donation by actively religious donors totaled $13,356, which was 16% more than the average total contribution of all donors" (Adelle Banks, "Study: Religious donors don't plan to cut back," *USA Today,* April 17, 2009).

22. Dr. Jerry Rankin, "No easy task to change the status quo," *Baptist Press,* June 4, 1997, http://www.bpnews.net/bpnews.asp?id=3449.

Chapter 4

1. Thomas Carlyle, "Oliver Cromwell: The Capture of Drogheda," *The Letters and Speeches of Oliver Cromwell,* ed. S. C. Lomas (London, 1904), 1:466–71, http://www.mc.maricopa.edu/programs/sai/syllabi/his254/drogheda.pdf.

2. Roger Cohen, "The Muck of the Irish," *New York Times,* June 19, 2008.

3. "Celtic Tiger," *Wikipedia,* http://en.wikipedia.org/wiki/Celtic_Tiger.

4. More than 1.5 million Irish people immigrated to the United States between 1845 and 1860 (Maura Jane Farrelly, "Historically Homogeneous Societies Challenged by Immigration," March 7, 2006, http://www.voanews.com/english/archive/2006-03/2006-03-07-voa74.cfm).

5. There is a massive backlash against the institutionalized church. Many evangelists now believe that only one-on-one evangelism works with Irish people, while street evangelism and mass rallies do not. A Catholic church in County Cork that used to attract one thousand worshippers for Saturday mass now sees less than one hundred people attend the service. One observer told me that the Catholic Church in Ireland was too wedded to the Irish government and nationalism, and since the culture has changed beneath it, the church has gone into a tailspin.

6. During the 1992 U.S. presidential campaign, the campaign staff of Arkansas Governor Bill Clinton decided to attack incumbent President George H. W. Bush on the basis of the then-faltering American economy. Polls showed that voters felt insecure about their financial futures and blamed President Bush. To keep campaign staffers on message, chief strategist James Carville posted a sign in Clinton's Little Rock, Arkansas, campaign headquarters. The sign read,

"THE ECONOMY, STUPID," to remind everyone that Clintonites wanted to focus on one issue and one issue only—the economy. During the campaign, all roads would lead to the economy. A paraphrase of that same slogan could be applied to Ireland during the early part of the twenty-first century: "It's Migration, stupid."

7. Trista Winnie, "Ireland Shaped by Growing Immigrant Population," Common Census Blog, March 17, 2008, http://www.nuwireinvestor.com/blogs/com-moncensus/2008/03/ireland-shaped-by-growing-immigrant.html

8. Nick Park, "Immigration, Citizenship & Nationhood," The New Ireland, May 2, 2007, http://nickpark.wordpress.com/2007/05/02/immigration-citizenship-nationhood/.

9. Migration takes many forms:

Transnational adoption: Since 1991, Americans have adopted thousands of Chinese children, at a cost of about $15,000 apiece. During the beginning of the twenty-first century, China was the top source for Americans seeking foreign adoptions, with 6,493 visas being granted to Chinese orphans in 2006 ("China Center of Adoption Affairs," *Wikipedia,* http://en.wikipedia.org/wiki/China_Center_of_Adoption_Affairs).

Short-term missions: Short-term mission trips from Western churches are also booming. The numbers are huge: In 1989, 120,000 American laypeople were involved in short-term projects; today that number has grown to over one million ("What's Happening in Short-Term Mission?" *Lausanne World Pulse,* March 2006, 25). Short-term missions began in the middle of the twentieth century aimed at mobilizing college graduates or young adults into mission work. With increasing awareness of needs and opportunities in other countries, around the world there has been a surge in vision beyond national borders.

Tourism: Tourism is up. Eight hundred and forty-two million people traveled the globe as tourists in 2006, the highest number of international tourist arrivals in history ("World Tourism Sets Record in 2006," *AP Online,* January 29, 2007). Since the 1960s, international tourism has increased sevenfold. The most traveling occurred in Asian and Pacific countries, with the lowest level of international tourism occurring in Europe.

Study abroad: Any parent of a U.S. college student knows about the increasing popularity of—and opportunity for—studying abroad. In China alone, around 400,000 students are studying abroad at any given time, many paid for by the state. In 2004 and 2005, the number of American students studying abroad hit a record 205,983, more than double the number from ten years earlier ("Report on International Educational Exchange," Institute of Interational Education, http://opendoors.iienetwork.org/?p=113282, 2007). In 2009 there were a reported 103,260 Indian students in the United States ("Top Countries of Origin of Foreign Students in the United States," *The Chronicle of Higher Education*, November 16, 2009).

Pilgrimages: In 2005, over 1.1 million pilgrims performed the Hajj, making an international pilgrimage to Mecca in Saudi Arabia. Of those, 1,021,171 pilgrims arrived by air, 70,019 by road, and 17,457 by sea (Galal Fakkar, "Haj Preparations Complete," *Arab News*, January 1, 2006, http://www.arabnews.com/?page=1&section=0&article=75569&d=1&m=1&y=2006).

Conflict: In 2006, 24.5 million people around the world physically had to leave their homes to escape oppression, earning them the charming bureaucratic label of "internally displaced persons" (IDPs). That same year, almost four million Colombians were displaced due to civil war between right-wing paramilitaries and leftist guerrillas over control of drug trafficking routes. Other countries with high numbers of IDPs were Sudan (5 million), Uganda (1.7 million), and Iraq (1.7 million) ("Internal Displacement," Internal Displacement Monitoring Centre, http://www.internal-displacement.org/8025708F004CFA06/(httpPublications)/6F9D5C47FA0DCCE2C1257 2BF002B9212?OpenDocument).

Natural disaster: Other migrants are displaced not by governments but by nature. The tragic truth behind natural disasters is that they disproportionately affect impoverished residents of global south countries, where physical infrastructure and social services are so inadequate. In 2007, almost 20 million people were displaced as floods hit a wide swath of northern India, Bangladesh, and Nepal ("Devastating floods hit South Asia," *BBC News*, August 3, 2007, http://news.bbc.co.uk/1/hi/world/south_asia/6927389.stm). On December 26, 2004, the Asian tsunami resulted in 1,126,900 people displaced and 14,100 people missing ("2004 Indian Ocean earthquake," *Wikipedia*, http://en.wikipedia.org/wiki/2004_Indian_Ocean_earthquake). In 2008, an earthquake in China killed 68,000 people and left at least 4.8 million homeless ("2008 Sichuan earthquake," *Wikipedia*, http://en.wikipedia.org/wiki/2008_Sichuan_earthquake).

10. Giovanna Marconi, "Urban inclusion of international migrants: a further challenge for the cities of the South," Universitia Iuav di Vinezia.

11. Because it is "an international symbol of the migratory phenomenon," Spain was chosen as host of the Second World Social Migrations Forum in 2006. Over a million foreigners immigrated to Spain in 2003 and 2004, and 650,000 arrived in 2005—twice the level of the second-highest EU nation.

12. Alicia Fraerman, "Immigration—Spain: No Way to Fence Off the Sea," *Inter Press Service News Agency,* May 8, 2006, http://ipsnews.net/print.asp?idnews=33166. Their journeys are often dramatic, indeed. During the spring in 2006, Spanish authorities one weekend intercepted more than five hundred people who arrived in Spain in canoes and pateras (low-floating boats), mostly from Mauritania and Morocco. The Civil Guard's radar picked up another patera with sixty-two migrants aboard, two miles south of the Canary Island of Tenerife. Over the course of three days, authorities picked up 945 undocumented immigrants. But even while thousands of immigrants are either intercepted or successful in their efforts, many do not make it. In April 2005, thirty-two immigrants drowned when their boat sank off the coast of Mauritania. Spain's interior minister announced plans for Spain to assist Tenerife by providing an electronic surveillance system, complete with mobile units, to detect "irregular maritime immigration" and "variations in migratory routes."

13. Ibid.

14. Conference organizers could have chosen to stage the conference anywhere in the world, so they chose Spain: a country near the Muslim world and "the 10/40 window." This term, coined by Luis Bush in 1990, describes the area of the world between the 10th and 40th parallels on the map. Missions researchers have identified that 2,500 of the world's "unreached people groups" live in this area. As a result, much strategy and effort and mobilization by mission agencies around the world has focused on the 10/40 window.

    Further, the conference organizers knew that Latin American missionaries could get there without impossible expense or undue visa problems. In the conference sessions themselves, mobility and migration of people were assumed, and distinctions like "the sending world" and "the mission field" were blurred.

15. Columbus had courted Queen Isabella's support persistently over the years and was devastated when she initially turned him down at their 1492 meeting. Leaving town in failure, he was overtaken on the outskirts of town by the

King's soldiers and summoned back to the palace for further discussion. They went on to strike a deal. Columbus had been fortunate enough to intersect with one of history's great patrons of exploration and missions.

16. Delno C. West and August J. Kling, *The Libro de las Profecias of Christopher Columbus* (Gainesville, FL: University of Florida Press, 1991). It seems that a large part of Columbus' motivation for discovering the New World was spiritual. His "case statement" for Queen Isabella, based on a compilation of prophecies from the Old and New Testament and other sources, argued that his voyages would usher in a last age with a Last World Emperor, who would recapture the holy apocalyptic city of Jerusalem and initiate a messianic period. He suggested that he would discover gold in the Indies that could be used to conquer Jerusalem.

17. From the Columbus statue, I walked north on the Street of Catholic Kings, past ancient Arab neighborhoods and bazaars, and up a winding cobblestone road to El Alhambra. El Alhambra is a stunning castle and the symbol of Granada. When the occupying Moors completed El Alhambra in 1390, it stood as a showy symbol of Muslim military and cultural dominance. When the Christian Spanish forces finally routed the Moors out of Spain in the Battle of Granada in 1492, it capped a very good year for Queen Isabella and King Ferdinand, for that was also the year that Columbus would discover America. The Moors were dominant in Spain for eight centuries, and El Alhambra was the pinnacle of Muslim western expansion. To this day "Al Andalus"—the Arabic name given to the Iberian peninsula—reminds Muslims of that era when people throughout Europe looked to Muslim southern Spain for the best in medicine, philosophy, engineering, architecture, and culture.

18. Many Spaniards feel that immigration is one of their country's worst problems. In 2005, the socialist government offered amnesty to six hundred thousand illegal immigrants, which served to fuel mounting resentment. One year after the amnesty, there were already one million new undocumented foreigners living in Spain.

19. While in Granada, I met an Egyptian man sent by the fabulous Cairo church Kasr El Dobara to be a missionary in Barcelona, Spain. He told me that, out of 44 million people in Spain, only 100,000 of them were evangelical Christians. Because of the massive migration of people, half of all those evangelicals were Latin Americans. Latin American immigrants were streaming into Spain,

he said, mostly for economic opportunity. That Migration caused a division among Spain's small evangelical communities—indigenous Spaniards and expatriate whites (Americans, British, or Germans) on the one hand and poor immigrant "cousins" from Latin America (whom Spaniards tended to look down upon) on the other.

20. David Whitehouse, "Half of Humanity Set to Go Urban," *BBC News,* May 19, 2005, http://news.bbc.co.uk/2/hi/science/nature/4561183.stm.

21. George Packer, "The Megacity," *New Yorker,* November 13, 2006.

22. The dark, Dickensian view of cities is captured in one writer's description of the Nigerian megacity, Lagos:

> Newcomers to the city are not greeted with the words "Welcome to Lagos." They are told "This is Lagos"—an ominous statement of fact…. [A] worker in one of the sawmills along the lagoon, said, "We understand this as 'Nobody will care for you, and you have to struggle to survive.'" It is the singular truth awaiting the six hundred thousand people who pour into Lagos from West Africa every year. Their lungs will burn with smoke and exhaust; their eyes will sting; their skin will turn charcoal gray. And hardly any of them will ever leave. (Packer, "The Megacity," *New Yorker,* November 13, 2006)

23. One of the global church's most pressing challenges in the twenty-first century will be establishing Christian ministry in the world's largest cities, especially in the non-Christian, non-Western world (Patrick Johnstone and Jason Mandryk, *Operation World—21st Century Edition* [Carlisle, UK: Paternoster Lifestyle, 2001], 710).

24. Andy Crouch, *Culture Making* (Downer's Grove, IL: InterVarsity Press, 2008).

25. That designation was first employed in 1974 by Dr. Ralph Winter, a professor at Fuller Seminary in Pasadena, California, to refer to tribes and ethnicities around the world that have never been exposed to the Christian message ("Ralph D. Winter," *Wikipedia,* http://en.wikipedia.org/wiki/Ralph_D._Winter).

26. John Bjorlie, "Five Missionary Martyrs," PlymouthBrethren.org, September 17, 2006, http://www.plymouthbrethren.org/article/545. The result was a sandbar ambush that left all five dead.

27. Tim Keller, *The Reason for God* (New York: Penguin Group, 2008).

28. Migration to cities continues "even when internal migrants became well aware of the difficult insecurity of tenure, scarce or no access to basic services, high levels of crime and violence, marginalization in the labor market and exclusion from many other social, civic and political opportunities" (Geovanna Marconi, "Urban inclusion of international migrants: a further challenge for the cities of the South.").

29. "Report of the Third Session of the World Urban Forum," UN-Habitat, June 19–23, 2006, 68.

30. Ibid.

31. In March 2006, eighty half-naked jungle dwellers realized that their trek had come to an end as they fearfully dragged into the hot, dusty town of San José del Guaviare, Columbia. The Nukak-Makú people had lived a Stone Age life since time immemorial, and this was their first-ever encounter with the modern world. After wandering two hundred miles from their remote jungle homeland, children and pet monkeys in tow, they literally ran out of cover. Over three hundred of the Nukak—about half of that tribe's estimated population—would end up in the town, fleeing from the kidnappings, massacres, and terror of Columbia's cocaine-fueled forty-year civil war. After centuries of fishing, weaving, and hunting monkeys in the jungle with poison-tipped blow darts, they went on to live the lives of refugees in internally displaced person camps. (Juan Forero, "Leaving the Wild, and Rather Liking the Change," *New York Times,* May 11, 2006.)

32. Lausanne Committee for World Evangelism, "Globalization and the Gospel: Rethinking Mission in the Contemporary World," Lausanne Occasional Paper No. 30 (September 29–October 5, 2004). Edilberto Gonzalez is my barber in Richmond. He arrived in Richmond in 2000, having finally seen his name move to the top of a mammoth waiting list to immigrate to the United States from his hometown of Camaguay, Cuba. When Eddy first started cutting my hair, his command of English was, to say the least, minimal. My hair needs are distressingly simple, though, so that was not a problem for either of us! He is unfailingly friendly and upbeat, and I found his immigrant story irresistible.

Eddy and I have since become good friends, and I have brought him souvenirs back from Cuba (for the record, I cannot recall whether any of them were tobacco products), given him Spanish children's books when Jonathan and Emmanuel were born, and eaten at his in-laws' excellent Cuban restaurant.

I taught Eddy how to say the English "y" that confounds Cubans, helping him pronounce the color "yellow" instead of "jello."

I love people from other countries, and am a strong believer in the distinctly American "melting pot" concept. Every month or so, my visit with Eddy reminds me of the great hope that immigrants place in the United States. It makes me thankful for the unique ways—however imperfectly—in which America embodies Christian values. At its best, the United States fosters Christianity by practicing transparency, integrity, freedom of speech and religion, due process, and equality. Eddy (a Roman Catholic) and Muslims and other immigrants I know in Richmond share a deep appreciation for those bedrock American commitments.

Eddy is living the American dream, and what I find most inspiring is that he knows it. Recently, he mentioned that business was slow because of a downturn in the economy. I asked if that concerned him, and he breezily said, "Not at all. In Cuba, I cut hair all day for years, and the government paid me five dollars a week. People in the United States have no idea; I do not have problems. I am a rich man, every day, my friend."

33. Pico Iyer, *The Global Soul* (New York: Vintage, 2001).

34. Malcolm McGregor, "Called to the City," SIM 114 (2006).

Chapter 5:

1. "Nike graffiti ads in Singapore spark controversy," *The Star Online,* November 26, 2004.

2. Ibid.

3. Benjamin Barber, *Jihad vs. McWorld* (New York: Ballantine Books, 1996), 17.

4. Yum! China, http://www.yum.com/company/china.asp.

5. Liu Jie, "McDonald's growing in China," *China Daily,* September 9, 2008, http://www.chinadaily.com.cn/bizchina/2008-09/08/content_7007412.htm.

6. "Starbucks Celebrates 10 Years in China with Initiatives Benefiting the Present and Future," January 14, 2009, http://www.starbucks.com/aboutus/pressdesc. asp?id=975.

7. Nike was listed as #153 in Fortune's "Global 500" rankings. "Global 500," *Fortune,* July 1, 2008, http://money.cnn.com/magazines/fortune/global500/2008/snapshots/2184.html.

8. "Nike graffiti ads in Singapore spark controversy," *The Star Online.*

9. The Fay case shows us much more than just Singaporean values of cleanliness and decorum. Fay's case highlighted the radically different views between the Western world and its focus on individual rights, and Asia with its focus on collective welfare. Singaporeans strongly believe that their tough laws against anti-social crimes are what keep Singapore orderly and relatively crime-free. By law, vandalism gets three to eight lashes. "Toughness is considered a virtue here. The theory is that a person shouldn't get off on fancy argument," says a law professor at the National University of Singapore and nominated member of Parliament. America's legal system, he continues, "has gone completely berserk. They're so mesmerized by the rights of the individual that they forget that other people have rights too" (Alejandro Reyes, "Rough Justice: A Caning in Singapore Stirs Up a Fierce Debate About Crime and Punishment," *Asiaweek,* May 25, 1994).

   Many Singaporeans reject the high value that the West places on individual freedom and autonomy. "The Western cliché that it would be better for a guilty person to go free than to convict an innocent person is testimony to the importance of the individual. But an Asian perspective may well be that it is better that an innocent person be convicted if the common welfare is protected than for a guilty person to be free to inflict further harm on the community." In the West, an accused person is presumed to be innocent. In Singapore, some report that no such commitment exists today.

10. "Nike graffiti ads in Singapore spark controversy," *The Star Online.*

11. The cultural strip mining also extends to linguistics. Only sixty-five languages are spoken by more than 10 million people and only forty-five are used as a main teaching medium in secondary schools. Over fifty have one speaker only, 426 are nearly extinct and some estimate that half of the 7148 languages may be extinct in 2100 (Johnstone and Mandryk, *Operation World—21st Century Edition,* 10).

12. Corporations like Nike have enormous financial projections and international reach to match, so they conceive high-stakes marketing campaigns to reach far-flung cities, countries, and cultures. Nike's contract with the New York-based NBA guaranteed that both Nike and the NBA would spread their brands throughout Asia, from the tiniest Malaysian village to the dozens of Chinese cities with populations exceeding one million residents.

13. Iyer, *The Global Soul,* 24.

14. I was teaching a course in the Darjeeling district of northeast India, when Nukshi, a twentysomething university ministry leader, sidled up behind me singing the nonsensical-but-hilarious "Spiderpig" song from *The Simpsons Movie.* My daughter Evie was with me, and her jaw dropped in amazement.

15. Richard Flemming, "Missions: The New Realities," *Evangelical Baptist,* November– December 2003, http://www.christianity.ca/NetCommunity/Page.aspx?pid=4167.

16. Katherine Calos, "English becoming world's language," *Richmond Times-Dispatch,* November 1, 2007.

17. Ibid.

18. Geoffrey Nunberg, "Will the Internet Always Speak English?" *The American Prospect,* November 30, 2002, http://www.prospect.org/cs/articles?article=will _the_internet_always_speak_english.

19. Ibid.

20. Told to me by Peter Kuzmic at Evangelical Theological Seminary in Osijek, Croatia.

21. Dr. Mark Valeri taught that most Old Testament commentators explain Joseph's interpretation of Pharoah's dreams in Genesis 41 against the backdrop of the fact the Egyptian magicians interpreted dreams by using a "dream book," that provided interpretive keys to dream symbols. Joseph had been trained in Pharoah's court and clearly understood the training of the magicians. Because he understood the ways of both the magicians and God, Joseph was able to engage Pharoah with confidence and success. When he interpreted the dream, he was doing a very Egyptian thing. But he interpreted the dream correctly because God inspired his act of translation.

22. Tom W. Sine Jr., "Globalization, Creation of Global Culture of Consumption and the Impact on the Church and Its Mission," *Evangelical Review of Theology* 25.1 (October 2003).

Chapter 6:

1. "The ruling military junta changed its name from Burma to Myanmar in 1989, a year after thousands were killed in the suppression of a popular uprising. Rangoon also became Yangon. The Adaptation of Expression Law also introduced English language names for other towns, some of which were not

ethnically Burmese. The change was recognised by the United Nations, and by countries such as France and Japan, but not by the United States and the UK.... A statement by the Foreign Office says: 'Burma's democracy movement prefers the form 'Burma' because they do not accept the legitimacy of the unelected military regime to change the official name of the country. Internationally, both names are recognised.' So does the choice of Burma or Myanmar indicate a particular political position? Mark Farmener, of Burma Campaign UK, says: 'Often you can tell where someone's sympathies lie if they use Burma or Myanmar. Myanmar is a kind of indicator of countries that are soft on the regime.'" ("Should it be Burma or Myanmar?" *BBC News*, September 27, 2007, http://news.bbc.co.uk/1/hi/magazine/7013943. stm).

2. "Cyclone Nargis," *Wikipedia,* http://en.wikipedia.org/wiki/Cyclone_Nargis.

3. Michael Sullivan, "Myanmar's People Slide Deeper Into Despair," *NPR,* February 17, 2009, http://www.npr.org/templates/story/story.php?storyId=1 00639178&ft=1&f=1001.

4. "Burma," *Wikipedia,* http://en.wikipedia.org/wiki/Burma.

5. "Cyclone Nargis—One Year On: WorldVision's Response," WorldVision, http://wvasiapacific.org/downloads/Nargis_one_year_report.pdf.

6. Rebecca Lindsey, "NASA Satellite Captures Images of Cyclone Nargis Flooding in Burma," NASA, May 6, 2008, http://www.nasa.gov/topics/earth/features/nargis_floods.html.

7. Associated Press, "Cyclone Nargis embodied the 'perfect storm,'" *MSNBC,* May 8, 2008, www.msnbc.msn.com/id/24526960.

8. Ibid.

9. Burma's reclusive junta, nursing long-standing resentment over domination by Western governments, refused all outside aid for at least ten days after the cyclone ("India urges Myanmar to accept global aid, junta agrees," *Thaindian News,* May 13, 2008, http://www.thaindian.com/newsportal/uncategorized/india-urges-myanmar-to-accept-global-aid-junta-agrees-lead_10047982.html).

10. "How We Work," World Vision, 2009.

11. That was the opinion expressed to me by Justin Henriques, who founded and runs Least of These International, a ministry that meets basic needs of rural communities in developing countries through the use of appropriate and sustainable technologies.

12. Matthew 22:37–40: "Jesus said unto him, Thou shalt love the Lord thy God with all thy heart, and with all thy soul, and with all thy mind. This is the first and great commandment. And the second is like unto it, Thou shalt love thy neighbour as thyself. On these two commandments hang all the law and the prophets" (KJV).

13. Matthew 28:19–20: "Therefore go and make disciples of all nations, baptizing them in the name of the Father and of the Son and of the Holy Spirit, and teaching them to obey everything I have commanded you. And surely I am with you always, to the very end of the age."

14. Michael Jaffarian, "The Computer Revolution and Its Impact on Evangelical Mission Research and Strategy," *International Bulletin of Missionary Research* 33 (2009): 37.

15. Jonathan J. Bonk, "Movements, Missiometrics, and World Christianity," *International Bulletin of Missionary Research* 31 (2007): 1, quoted in Jaffarian, "The Computer Revolution and Its Impact on Evangelical Mission Research and Strategy," *International Bulletin of Missionary Research.*

16. Jaffarian, "The Computer Revolution and Its Impact on Evangelical Mission Research and Strategy," 34.

17. Ian Davis and Elizabeth Stephenson, "Ten Trends to watch in 2006," *The McKinsey Quarterly,* January 2006, http://www.mckinseyquarterly.com/Strategy /Globalization/Ten_trends_to_watch_in_2006_173.

18. Shane Hipps, *Flickering Pixels: How Technology Shapes Your Faith* (Grand Rapids, MI: Zondervan, 2009), 115.

19. Fort Sherman Academy, http://www.fortsherman.org/index.html.

20. Franklin Foer, "The Passion's Precedent: The Most-Watched Film Ever?" *New York Times,* February 8, 2004, http://www.nytimes.com/2004/02/08/ movies/08FOER.html.

21. John Brandon, "Crazy Passion," *Christianity Today,* October 2009, 42.

Chapter 7

1. "Hasyim Muzadi," *The international artist database,* September 23, 2003, http://www.culturebase.net/artist.php?1150.

2. Martin E. Marty and R. Scott Appleby, eds., *Fundamentalisms Comprehended* (Chicago: University of Chicago Press, 1995). One of several volumes from The Fundamentalism Project at the University of Chicago.

3. Gregory Paul and Phil Zuckerman, "Why the gods are not winning," *Edge,* April 30, 2007, http://www.edge.org/3rd_culture/paul07/paul07_index.html.

4. Robert D. Putnam, "*E Pluribus Unum:* Diversity and Community in the Twenty-First Century—The 2006 Johan Skytte Prize," *Scandinavian Political Studies* 30.2 (June 2007): 142.

5. Barber, *Jihad vs. McWorld,* quoted in Tom Sine, *Mustard Seed versus McWorld* (Grand Rapids, MI: Baker Books, 1999), 78.

6. Roger Cohen, "Bring the Real World Home," *New York Times*, November 12, 2007.

7. Ibid.

8. The April 2009 five-day standoff at sea between the United States Navy and a tiny band of Somali pirates is just one illustration.

9. Lausanne Committee for World Evangelism, "Globalization and the Gospel: Rethinking Mission in the Contemporary World," Lausanne Occasional Paper No. 30 (September 29–October 5, 2004). "[W]e should not be surprised to find that our evangelism and missions will be considered as simply one more form of globalism seeking to dominate others."

10. Frank Decker, "When 'Christian' Does Not Translate," *Mission Frontiers,* September–October 2005, 8.

11. David Brooks, "Questions of Culture," *New York Times,* February 19, 2006.

12. Iyer, *The Global Soul.*

13. Elias A. Zerhouni (Johns Hopkins University commencement address), quoted in Sam Dillon, "Commencement Speeches; Graduates Get an Earful from Left, Right and Center," *New York Times,* June 11, 2006.

14. One particularly audacious incident occurred in Karachi, Pakistan, amid persistent strife between Hindus and Muslims. Muslims eventually seized a Hindu temple. The Muslims proceeded to convert the temple into a slaughterhouse. Of course, this was one of the most offensive acts imaginable to Hindus, for whom the killing of cattle is strictly forbidden (Russell Working, "Hindus facing persecution," *Chicago Herald Tribune,* July 13, 2007).

15. Allen D. Hertzke, "Report on International Religious Freedom," Pew Charitable Trusts, 2009, 17.

16. Samuel Huntington, *The Clash of Civilizations* (New York: Simon & Schuster, 1998).

17. Johnstone and Mandryk, *Operation World—21st Century Edition*. India has around 130 million Muslim citizens and 800 million Hindus.

18. "Watchdog hails improved security in Malacca Strait," *The Straits Times*, January 23, 2007.

19. Craig S. Smith, "Christian Shepherd Shines His Light in Islamic Pasture," *New York Times*, July 22, 2006.

20. Hertzke, "Report on International Religious Freedom," 18.

21. Angel Rabasa, Cheryl Benard, Lowell H. Schwartz, and Peter Sickle, *Building Moderate Muslim Networks* (Santa Monica, CA: Rand Corporation, 2007), 1–2.

22. "Hasyim Muzadi," *The international artist database,* September 23, 2003, http://www.culturebase.net/artist.php?1150.

23. Aleksandr Solzhenitsyn, *The Gulag Archipelago,* (New York: Harper Perennial Modern Classics, 2002), 312. "It was only when I lay there on rotting prison straw that I sensed within myself the first stirrings of good. Gradually it was disclosed to me that the line separating good and evil passes not through states, not between classes, nor between political parties either—but right through every human heart—and through all human hearts. This line shifts. Inside us, it oscillates with the years. And even within hearts overwhelmed by evil, one small bridgehead of good is retained. And even in the best of hearts, there remains … an unuprooted small corner of evil. Since then I have come to understand the truth of all religions of the world: They struggle with the evil inside a human being (inside every human being). It is impossible to expel evil from the world in its entirety, but it is possible to constrict it within each person."

24. A predictable thing is happening as globalization spreads, like volcanic ash, to all corners of the earth, indiscriminately carrying the same message to all cultures: There is resistance and backlash. Cultures, countries, or people groups that do not give in to the global economy or international media or other types of globalization respond in several ways.

Sometimes they retreat from the modern culture and hide. They hope that the winds of change will blow by, leaving them unaffected. This sometimes works, for a while. The Shaker sect of the eighteenth century died off. The Amish still survive but constantly have to work harder to fend off assimilation.

In many parts of the world, people do not have the means—whether for lack of money or education—to keep up with their changing society. That can cause a case of "haves" and "have nots," which in turn breeds resentment and anger. In response to a feeling of being overwhelmed by forces outside of their control, many people around the world are seeking a return to old ways. They are digging their heels in. Surely, many Islamic terrorists voice condemnation of moderation, which they attribute to the West and to Christianity.

Sometimes they splinter. Different groups choose the aspects of their culture that they most dearly want to preserve, and they create subcultures based around those distinctions. Many parts of Ireland still look more like the nineteenth century than the twenty-first, once you get away from the cities. But then other parts are trending strongly toward modernism and away from tradition. Irish society is splintering. Singapore, too, is splintering. While distinctly Singaporean customs remain, modern culture is also eroding many traditions.

25. Wesley, induction address, http://www.nts.edu/induction-address-dr-david -wesley-winter-2006.

26. Martin E. Marty, *By Way of Response*, quoted in Richard J. Mouw, *Uncommon Decency: Christian Civility in an Uncivil World* (InterVarsity Press, 1992), 12.

27. Mouw, 12.

28. Eboo Patel, *Acts of Faith: The Story of an American Muslim, the Struggle for the Soul of a Generation* (Boston, MA: Beacon Press, 2007), 48, 51.

29. Ibid., xv.

30. Ibid., 166–67.

31. Ibid., 166.

32. Ibid., 161–165.

33. Mouw, 100–102.

34. Diana Eck, "World Religions, Diversity and Dialogue" (lecture), quoted in Ari L. Goldman, "A Newsman In Divinity School," *New York Times,* November 8, 1987.

35. Rob Moll, "The Father of Faith-Based Diplomacy," *Christianity Today,* September 2008.

36. "East-West Institute," *SourceWatch,* www.sourcewatch.org/index.php?title=East -West_Institute.

37. "December 2008 E-Update," The Becket Fund, December 16, 2008, www.becketfund.org/index.php/article/1065.html.

Chapter 8:

1. As estimated by the UN Population Division (http://www.aidsuganda.org/
   pdf/Uganda_HIV_profile_U_Calif.pdf).

2. Told to the author by Dr. Paul Marshall.

3. Kenya did not gain independence until 1963, but its robust tourist trade and
   Nairobi's status as an East African hub have created vibrancy and a flow of
   different ideas and people. Nigeria, another former British colony, has used its
   oil revenue and aggressive citizens to arrive at a kind of self-determinism that
   is the antithesis of postcolonial passivity. In war-ravaged nations like Rwanda,
   Burundi, and Sudan, wars have largely routed out reliance on old colonial
   habits and everything else. In a place like South Africa, free from British rule
   since 1994, there is enough international trade and free-market competition
   that people and institutions there thrive or fail based on today and not on
   traditions or patronages from their colonial era. The need to move beyond
   apartheid, too, has hastened South Africa's embrace of new ways.

4. Sudan, Tunisia, Morocco (1956), Ghana (1957), Guinea (1958), Cameroon,
   Togo, Mali, Senegal, Madagascar, DR Congo, Somalia, Benin, Niger, Burkina
   Faso, Cote d'Ivoire, Chad, Central African Republic, Congo, Gabon, Nigeria,
   Mauritania (1960), Sierra Leone, Tanzania (1961), Rwanda, Burundi, Algeria,
   Uganda (1962), Kenya (1963), Malawi, Zambia (1964), Gambia (1965),
   Botswana, Lesotho (1966) ("Decolonization of Africa," *Wikipeida,* http://
   en.wikipedia.org/wiki/Decolonisation_of_Africa).

5. Anthony Appiah and Henry Louis Gates, Jr., eds., *Africana: The Encyclopedia
   of the African and African American Experience* (New York: Basic Books, 1999).

6. For example, during Uganda's 2006 Presidential election an opposition candidate was suddenly and mysteriously jailed. In a gesture of protest against
   what appeared to be government interference in a democratic election, donor
   nations withheld around 70 million dollars in aid.

7. Samuel, an itinerant evangelist in his early twenties with a burning passion for
   youth, described for me how Memory persists strongly within younger circles.
   He volunteered that postcolonialism is a major factor in his generation, evident
   in the still-operating British education system instituted during colonial times.
   The British education model, in Uganda and so many other countries, emphasized instruction by lecture and learning by rote memorization. Many adult
   Ugandans feel that their education prepared them for jobs of servitude or civil

service—but not for entrepreneurialism or positions of initiative. (Incidentally, several generations of Indians would make the same claim about education during their country's eighty-nine years as a British colony.) They point to the expectations for students to be passive in educational settings, speaking only when spoken to and dutifully taking notes rather than asking questions or engaging in dialogue. Samuel told me that he was in the midst of a personal "youth tour." In search of a new way to reach African youth, he was traveling around and interviewing youth and youth workers. He was, like me, trying to find clues, and so far he had found two major ones.

First, youth ministry in Uganda needed to "reboot," in order to become current with the changing world that the youth are dying to enter. If he and others did not reinvent and update their methods, they would soon become irrelevant. That sounded familiar.

Second, he knew that any ministry outreach needed to be respectful of some core African ways that were not changing, such as their deep respect for parents and authorities. As an example, he said that he constantly asked himself whether new approaches he was considering would be pleasing to God and effective with his youth audience, as well as acceptable to his elders.

That was a difficult balance to strike: How to be hip enough to reach kids, but respectful enough to avoid threatening traditionally minded elders. He lamented that the common solution erred very much on one side: African youth workers often deferred to traditional African ways when communicating the gospel, but would not incorporate the fresh, new global ideas that so invigorated and captured Uganda youth in every other aspect of their lives.

8. Every citizen during the Soviet era lived multiple lives, revealing only incomplete slices of themselves at various times to different acquaintances, friends, family, or authorities. People who grew up during Soviet times—and their children after them—were not wholly known by anyone in their lives. One young woman acknowledged the psychological toll caused by a childhood of feeling fractured and incomplete.

Now, as she was beginning a career as a graphic artist, she wanted to trust God for a healthier future for her and her children. She told me that she had named her new design firm "Calder," after the famous British sculptor who invented "mobiles." Mobiles are sculptures suspended by wires from high places, like ceilings or balconies or roofs. Calder's mobiles were hanger-like frames balancing different amoeba-shaped plates that would drift and twist and twirl in air currents. To this woman, mobiles represented balance. It was balance, after all—with her professional, social, religious, and personal lives lived in openness—that she most craved in her life in post-Soviet Russia. She seemed neither confident nor pessimistic about her ability to achieve that balance.

As a result of that rich time of asking questions and listening, I got a glimpse into the deep psychological and emotional damage carried by children of the former Soviet Union. For instance, future mission workers entering into discussions about God the Father with people in former Communist countries must first explain why the biblical image of "Father" is trustworthy and loving and not that of a harsh dictator.

9. In a study in contrasts, on my flight back to the States, the headline in a full-page *USA Today* ad blared "WHY BLEND IN?" Leaders in the United States are cultivated and highly esteemed. Both secular and Christian institutions focus intensively on molding young people into mature leaders.

10. As told to the author by Anita Deyneka, October 5, 2009.

11. *Ukraine,* A World Bank Country Study (Washington DC: The World Bank, 1999), 6.

12. Dr. Bent Fulton, quoted in Ralph Ennis, *An Introduction to the Mainland Chinese Soul,* http://www.leadconsulting-usa.com/index.php?main_page =product_info&cPath=2&products_id=2.

13. One example of cultural differences in business is between the Middle Eastern countries and the Western countries, especially the United States. When negotiating in Western countries, the objective is to work toward a target of mutual understanding and agreement and "shake hands" when that agreement is reached—a cultural signal of the end of negotiations and the start of "working together." In Middle Eastern countries, much negotiation takes place leading into the "agreement," signified by shaking hands. However, the deal is not complete in the Middle Eastern culture. In fact, it is a cultural sign that "serious" negotiations are just beginning. Imagine the problems this creates when each party in a negotiation is operating under diametrically opposed "rules and conventions." This is just one example why it is critical to understand other cultures you may be doing business with—whether you're on a vacation in a

foreign country or negotiating a multimillion-dollar deal for your company (www.geert-hofstede.com).

Conclusion:

1. Christine Rosen, "The Age of Egocasting," *New Atlantis* 7 (Fall 2004/Winter 2005), 51–72.

2. In Brazil, the Mosers met another American missionary family, the Piersons, whose son Paul became a dean and professor of history and Latin American studies at Fuller Seminary in Pasadena, California. I interviewed Dr. Pierson on May 6, 2009.

3. Matthew Henry, *Commentary on the Whole Bible* (Grand Rapids, MI: Zondervan, 1961), 441.